PATH

to

BROKEN DREAMS

Annie Murphy

Pen Press Publishers Ltd

First published in Great Britain by
Pen Press Publishers Ltd
39-41, North Road
Islington
London N7 9DP

ISBN 1-904754-20-1

Printed and bound in the UK

A catalogue record of this book is available from the British
Library

Cover design Jaqueline Abromeit

Contents

Annie, Danno and Bernie

Grandma Murphy with Annie and Bernie in 1943

Annie and Danno, 1946

Leo (right) with his friend Tony Dunne, 1952

WOMEN AND GIRLS FROM ST. JOSEPH'S SCHOOL
WHO DIED IN SUMMERHILL AND WERE BURRIED IN DRUM CEMETERY

NAME	DATE	AGE	NAME	DATE	AGE
MARY ELLEN O'KEEFFE	1882	11	JOSEPHINE MURRAY	1897	9
MARY MARGARET DUFFICY	1883	6½	MARGARET NAUGHTON	1897	18
HANNAH WALSH	1884	8	NORAH SHANNON	1897	13
MARY McLOUGHLIN	1885	12	EVELINE BURKE	1897	10
MARY GERAGHTY	1885	11	GERTRUDE MORRISON	1897	3
MARGARET McGOWAN	1885	11	THERESA CURLEY	1898	12
MARY ANNE COGHLAN	1896	14	JANE TYRRELL	1898	8
LILLY MARGARET WHITE	1887	3	KATE O'MALLEY	1898	14
MARY STAUNTON	1887	15	LIZZIE O'CONNOR	1904	20
ELIZABETH O'CONNOR	1889	8	MARY CASEY	1912	4
SARAH McEVOY	1889	33	MARY SOMERS	1915	10
BRIDGET FLEMING	1889	16	MARY JO McPARTLAND	1917	12
KATE FLANNERY	1890	16	ELIZABETH NEILL	1918	16
ELLEN MURRAY	1890	4	MOLLIE IGO	1922	7
ANNE SMITH	1891	2	MARY THERESA REDDY	1925	3
MARY ANNE MURPHY	1891	22	MARGARET CROGHAN	1925	15
MARGARET FLANNERY	1892	18	LILY McMAHON	1930	7½
KATE MURRAY	1894	14	EILEEN KEENA	1933	2½
MARY SMITH	1895	10	MARY JANE BOYHAN	1940	7
MARY DOYLE	1895	12	PATRICIA LYNCH	1941	3
BRIDGET LENNON	1895	14	HANNAH MARY COFFEY	1945	9
MARY ELIZABETH DOYLE	1895	16	MARY BERNADETTE HEALY	1945	3
MARY ANNE O'SHEA	1895	11	MARY CHRISTINA NOONE	1946	5
ANNE HANLEY	1896	11	MARY TERESA HARRIS	1948	5½
MARY BURKE	1896	11	MARJORIE McNIECE	1949	60
MARY GREENE	1896		MARY BRIGID SHERLOCK	1952	18½

may they rest in peace

This stone was erected by a generous local couple and
not by any religious or government order.

Entance to hell

I recall sitting on the doorstep of the house we shared with our Paternal Grandma in St. Vincents Street, Inchicore, Dublin.

I was curious as to who the stranger was who had just entered our street from Emmet Road where the number 21 bus had just stopped.

The man swapped his holdall bag from one hand to the other and crossed over to our side of the road. I had tried hard not to stare as he neared our door and was surprised when he gestured with his hand that he wanted me to move out of his way. It was not long before curiosity got the better of me and I went upstairs to where the man was fussing over Bernie (my little sister, Bernadette) and chatting to Mam and Gran. My father had joined the RAF when I was four, so I did not remember him.

My parents Eileen and Leo had married in May 1936; my father had gone away when Danno, my older brother was five, I was four and Bernadette three. Our father was on leave before his posting to Colombo, but how long he was home I cannot recall, nor the birth of my new brother (also called Leo) the following June in 1945.

Apparently, due to many serious bouts of malaria, my father's stay abroad did not last long and he returned to field hospitals in England and eventually was stationed in Aldergrove in Northern Ireland. He did not make it home for Gran's funeral in March 1946, but his brother Mick and sisters Molly and Agnes did come over from England with their spouses who had all emigrated years before.

We apparently had met these relatives and our cousins before, but I had not remembered; the fact that it was a funeral that had brought our meeting was neither here nor there, it was just great to meet them and very sad when they returned to England.

Dad did eventually come home on leave and spent most of his time going to the pub, but worse still was he and Mam were not getting along very well. It emerged that the reason the RAF could not let him know of Gran's death was the fact that he was on leave, but not at home with us.

Gran had suffered greatly before her death at the age of sixty-nine, so her passing was seen as a relief. I can still recall her constantly calling out my mam's name both day and night.

I still felt sad not seeing her in her bed in the corner and would miss her dry humour. Her kitchen was always a hive of activity at Christmas time and she always allowed us to stay up very late at night as she and Mam prepared the food for Christmas day.

She was every bit the real Matriarch with a glass of stout by her hand and giving advice and orders – respect of our elders in those days was very much the norm.

Gran's kitchen was much larger than ours on the ground floor, but my favourite room was her parlour and nothing was going to dampen my plans to explore every inch of it, something Gran never permitted.

Another room on my list would be Uncle Dan's, he was my dad's brother and his room had a very interesting looking trunk in it. There was an understanding that Dan would always have a room with us until we were rehoused by the Corporation.

Another thing we had to accept was another of Dad's brothers coming to Gran's parlour every Sunday morning to listen to the wireless. Uncle Bill had a wife and family and lived nearby, but they did not have a wireless. He spent most of his visit telling us to be quiet, I was always glad when he left.

Uncle Dan was a soldier in the Irish Army, so was not home during the week. He was a man of few words, as was Uncle Bill and another of Dad's brothers, Paddy, who lived in the city; there were two others – Joe and Mick who had emigrated to England.

Uncle Dan was very much a confirmed bachelor but that is not saying he did not have lady admirers, one in particular called Minnie is the most memorable albeit for the wrong reasons. She was the butt of many a snigger from neighbours because her pursuit of Uncle Dan's affection fell on hollow ground.

I became fascinated with the photographs of ancestors hanging on Gran's parlour wall, especially the one of Grandad, he must have died when we were very young, or before we were born. His picture portrayed a man of small stature wearing gaiters and standing next to a coach and horses; he may have been employed by Gran's parents, apparently they had been in the transport trade and in their day it would have been horse-drawn carriages.

Judging by the impressive clothing worn by some of the relatives I would definitely not say that they looked poor. I suppose poverty could have come later, though we were by no means the poorest people in our neighbourhood.

I can still see the beige and green leaved lino on the parlour floor and the grand table with matching chairs in the middle of the room.

I loved the black metal fireplace with matching surround and the metal and brass fender. On either side of the tiled hearth stood two large sea shells.

The mantlepiece was covered in deep green brocade with gold tassels and the unusual ornaments had been made by family – the most attractive to me were the brass ladies shoes, I loved polishing them.

In the far corner of the room was a French-styled sofa in green leather that matched the seat covering on the dining chairs, and the legs on all furniture were unusually shaped.

Under the sash window stood Auntie Molly's Singer sewing machine, it too was covered in brocade; she was Dad's favourite sister and would use the machine on some of the occasions she visited on her holidays from England.

She also kept precious toys and a china doll and china tea set locked in Gran's sideboard; she never allowed me to look closely at them, she inspected them on all of her visits, they were to be kept for passing on to the daughter she hoped to have. I had tried many times to unlock the door with keys borrowed from various friends for a closer look, but to no avail.

First Holy Communion Day

This event was to be no less a great for Danny and myself simply because we were poor. Mam had scrimped and saved for Danny's suit and my dress and veil. I know my dress cost nineteen and six and the veil one and eleven pence, that was not cheap for the period.

Molly again came to the rescue with the making of my brown coat which was not to my liking, I would have liked a lighter colour and also shiny shoes rather than the serviceable ones I had to accept. Mam said they would last longer. I have to say that as usual Molly's skill showed in my coat, it had been one of her own but she made it a perfect fit. However, I made sure that I did get a say when choosing the white shoulder bag.

To be honest it was not the religious aspect of the occasion that caused our excitement, it was the tradition that went with it. I had stood and let Mam curl my hair with hot tongs from the range, I suffered many burns for the big day.

It was customary for everyone you met on that day to contribute money to the children who had received Christ for the first time.

The visit to every known relative was next on the agenda and the journey to Mam's family home was to be looked forward to as Gran was bound to have made a special cake for the occasion. Most of Mam's brothers still lived at home as did one of her younger sisters, Lily. She was very religious and though she was always good to us she made that day memorable; I loved her with all my being, she was special for me.

Drudgery was far from my mind on that special day, I was almost certain that I could persuade Auntie Lily to let me have a go on her bike – I had tried on many occasions before and her answer was always the same, 'when you are bigger.'

Eight years old was late for First Holy Communion, it was usually taken aged seven, the age of reason according to Catholic teaching, I can only guess that Mam could not afford the cost at the right time.

Auntie Lily worked at the local paper mill as did other members of Mam's family and she popped in to see us quite regularly, always riding her green bike. She ran a clothes club and collected the weekly payments from various local people. I do not know if Lily was aware that Mam was not always with us when she visited or if she would have discussed it with the rest of Mam's family; it was to be much later in time that I became aware that Mam's family were not happy with Mam's choice of husband, it was apparent by their absence whenever Dad was home. I was also to learn that even Dad's own mother had warned Mam that she would rue the day she met Dad.

I cannot recall exactly when life became stressful for us, only that things got worse as Dad's leave became more frequent after his transfer to Aldergrove; he was released from the Royal Airforce Voluntary Reserve in August 1946 but re-enlisted in the Regular Air Force in the end of 1946 just days before Christmas.

As I was too young to know anything about my father for the first six years of my life, I can make no judgement of what kind of man he was, but I was beginning to dislike the man who started to beat my Mam, using her like a punchbag.

As kids we received little in the way of affection and the little fuss we did get was always from Mam, though she could be heavy-handed at times.

I had always played a big part in helping Mam to look after my little brother Leo but things got harder when our new sister arrived on August 22nd 1947.

Sheila's arrival is clear in my mind as I recall the neighbours putting little Leo in the pram and ordering me and Bernadette to take him to the park and telling us not to hurry back. We trotted off with sandwiches and bottles of water and obeyed the ladies who were on call for the home birth – they were the days when children obeyed all elders, whether related or not. I remember the male doctor and the dark-skinned lady who accompanied him getting off the bus; they both carried bags, they had come from the Coombe hospital in the City.

I do not recall seeing our brother Danny (sometimes called Danno) anywhere that day – he was quite good at disappearing, especially when it came to anything domestic.

As we killed time in the park, I wondered if there was a

chance that either of the doctors would have brought us a black baby. We had always been led to believe that one day when we had put enough pennies in the box at school for African babies we would actually buy one. Seeing the dark-skinned lady arriving and the fact that one of the neighbours who had sent us off for the day had informed me that by the time I got home I would have another brother or sister in the house, adding up all the clues led me to the conclusion that it could be an African baby.

You have to understand that Mam's getting rounder in those days did not suggest that babies were on the way, nor did people talk about such things – babies appeared in homes, children did not question where they came from.

Little could I have known how much harder my life would become after the arrival of Sheila.

I cannot recall just how long it was before Mam started going out and leaving me to mind the smaller kids, but I was given far too much responsibility for my age, especially when it came to the welfare of two very young children – I was becoming like a little mother.

Acting As Mother Was Hard

Mam's habit of leaving me to play mother was becoming too frequent and she was leaving us for longer periods, sometimes overnight and on occasions from Friday night to late on Sunday.

Luckily Sheila was a good baby and was easily pacified but Leo was hard work; I found it very hard and worried what would happen in the event of an accident, I never had a clue as to where Mam was.

I have no memories of Dad taking Mam out with him when he came home on leave; I don't know if he ever wrote and informed Mam that he was coming home, though I know he wrote more letters when he was stationed abroad, they always ended with 'give my love to the kids.' It was only words, the only kind of love we knew was the kind we kids had for each other.

We bigger kids had a special bonding and in our own way loved the little ones. Danny was a free spirit who appeared at feeding time and disappeared again as quick, he took no part in the domestic side of life.

I did not spend every day in misery, I have memories of normality, well as normal as possible. I enjoyed the time I had free to be a child, it is just unfortunate that the bad memories have lingered.

I was always scared for Mam at the risks she was taking when she stayed away overnight, for fear that Dad would come and find us on our own. He was a man who would beat her for simply answering him back and would hit her hard enough to loosen teeth for looking at him sideways.

She was far from being a good mam, but I suffered each time she took a beating from Dad; she was my mam and I loved her.

Much as I hated Mam's neglect of us, I hated Dad's leave more.

No Affection, No Cuddles

As I have already said we received very little outward show of affection from either parent, though Dad did show feelings towards Bernadette.

I remember times during Dad's leave when he played horseback rides with her and saw him kiss and hug her. I feel almost embarrassed to admit that there was an occasion when Dad was fussing over Bernadette because she had fallen and hurt herself. This gave me an idea, which I put to the test at a later date. I threw myself down the last few stairs expecting the same show of concern, I was careful not to cause anything too serious, I did not want to feel pain.

Dad did come to see what the fuss was about but ordered me to take more care on the stairs.

I cannot really say that I was overly disappointed at his lack of concern for me, I suppose I was used to having no attention, like the day he came home on leave in the earlier days and told

7

me to get off the doorstep and go sit on my own doorstep – he had not even recognised me. That did hurt my feelings.

Mam also rarely hit Bernadette as she did Danno and I always assumed it was because she was delicate, though I later wondered if it was because of the fear of Dad finding out and this would result in Mam herself getting battered for it. But no matter what, we still loved our little sister and did not want to see her smacked nor did we begrudge her any attention she got.

Mam's Blood-Soaked Clothing

One of the most fearful times of my life took place one night while the other kids slept. It was before the downstairs kitchen had been converted into a bedroom for Danno and Leo. We all still slept in the same large room. I was woken by noises from the kitchen upstairs – another beating was on the cards for Mam.

She had stayed up to cook Dublin coddle for Dad who would expect that on his return from the pub; he was on home leave. There was never any loud shouting, just dull sounds and then thumps on the floor or walls, then the sound of Mam pleading with Dad not to hit her.

Many times she would say, "that's enough, I can't take any more." It was in vain this night as it always was.

The hall light was on and I saw Mam's silhouette appear in the doorway, she had got away from Dad's grip and felt she would be safe from any more beatings if she got into bed. He was not likely to beat her if we were in the same room, so she was safe unless he dragged her out again. Though he never laid a hand on us children, he was still capable of rendering us speechless with fear.

Mam had a scar on the centre of her nose, that was re-opened more than once, though most of her injuries were out of sight – either on her body or her head.

The memory of Mam's clothing soaking in the tin bath is still vivid, the water was always red with her blood. Perhaps one day I may be able to forgive, but I will only forget when I am no longer capable of thought.

I have often wondered why Uncle Dan never came to Mam's rescue, his leave from the Irish Army was much more frequent than Dad's, and on many of the nights when Dad beat Mam, Dan would be in bed. I would rather believe that he was so well jarred he heard nothing, than think that he would (as many men of that era did) believe that women needed to be kept in their place. I really do not want to believe badly of Dan, he was very generous to us kids.

I have heard it said many times that men who beat women are cowards and would not pick on another man, but this was not the case with my father – he had no fear of anyone, no matter what their size, even though he himself was of small stature.

I have heard comments from various members of family suggest that Dad's strength came with him verging on madness, but not knowing about such things I am still convinced he was simply born with a very nasty streak.

I learned much later in life that we had had another brother who was born sometime between Bernie and Leo, he only lived a couple of days. Mam was convinced he died as the result of Dad beating and kicking her when she was eight months pregnant.

The baby was christened Anthony and apparently that is why Mam gave my little brother Leo the name Anthony as a second name when he was christened.

During many of the times in my life when I wonder what would have happened 'if only' this that or the other, I find myself wishing that Dad had never returned to our lives – after all better men than he had never returned from the war.

Mam's Short Fuse

There was never a time when it was possible to sit and chat to Mam and express my dislike of the things I did not think I should be asked to do but, looking back, I would not have imagined her ever being able to sit and have friendly chats with her mother – she also had never received affection; her mam and

9

dad did not get on very well, but the difference was that it was Granny who ruled and was quite capable of holding her own.

Mam had a very short fuse and let rip at us kids for the slightest of reasons, such as one of us tutting when asked to do some chore or errand. One of the things I hated most was having to go to one of the local shops and ask for credit.

I have vivid memories of Mam chasing me down the street for refusing to ask for credit. I would stay away from the house for hours until I thought she would have cooled down, I was not brave enough to stand and take the punishment for disobedience.

Mam very often belted us, and just when you thought it was over she would grab you as you walked away and give us another belting for something we had done the week before. Though she could rightly be classed as a child batterer, she was no different to thousands of Irish mothers of that era.

I also have memories of very touching and tender moments, like one night after she had given Danny a terrible beating. He was lying in bed, fast asleep with his mouth wide open as usual. Mam had assumed we were all asleep and went over to where he lay, she gently stroked his face and, with tears running down her face, softly whispered that she was sorry and would not do it again. I know she meant it, she always did, I also knew she would do it again and again and again.

She was never aware that I witnessed those precious moments that I have treasured my whole life. I suffered all pain inflicted on any member of my family, it hurt more than the actual pain I felt from a physical beating on my own body.

My Street And Our Neighbours

My world was in the street where we lived, though I could find my way to the city and to various relatives scattered about in different parts of Dublin.

The canal ran across the top of our street and there was a foot-walk across the canal lock which we often used to walk to Kimmage, where our gran on Mam's side lived.

As you walked towards the top of our street, we were divided from a place called 'Keogh Square' by a tall stone wall on the left-hand side, it went almost the whole length of the street. There was a lane that followed the wall to the left and the cemetery ran along the right side of the lane.

We called it Gypsy lane as there were travellers camping there more often than not. I was scared of their dogs and would not take the lane as a short cut to the lock. I preferred to go to the very top of the street and walk along the river path.

Keogh Square was known locally as 'The Barracks' and was enclosed behind a tall wall, with arch-shaped entrances. There was one entrance at the far end of our street, we did not enter there very much. It was said to have been an army establishment in the past. There was also rumour that it was the original 'Artane Boys School'. I could not vouch for that though, I had only ever known it as a place to house the very poor people of Dublin.

Goldenbridge Convent School was on the right-hand side of the top of the street and behind it stood an Orphanage. We attended the convent school; my attendance record was not good. I always had the feeling that local people were watching out for us during Mam's absences, especially Mrs Reid in number twelve.

The Creepy House On The Corner

Mam's absence from home did not affect Danno or Bernie as they could still play out as normal, though Bernie usually stayed around to help me.

I resented the loss of my childhood, but took every opportunity while Mam was around to pursue my favourite pastime of listening to ghost stories – daytime was for skipping and hopscotch but evening was special.

Yards from our house was a three-storey house, the front was on our street and it turned the corner to a place called Tram Terrace. There was an entrance to the large place in front and on the side, and even though it was all attached one end was called 'The Eagle House', and the other 'Cragans' – this was the exciting end.

There was a family on the second floor called Cragan but they did not own the building. Perhaps they were the longest tenants living there and the place just got called after them, I don't know the history.

There was a really creepy cellar under the building which was not used by any of the tenants, this was the special place where few kids would venture. It was pitch black below and with several of the steps missing, care had to be taken when entering or leaving. The floor was only clay and the light on summer evenings would shine through the old holes in the thick stone walls. From within we could look out on to communal clothes lines. Our only light on dark nights was from the candles we would light and our seats were big old rocks that were strewn around. Most of the kids who attended the meetings were boys – the girls were too scared. I was always wanting to prove how brave I was. Each person would take their turn to tell the latest scary story and the flickering candlelight added to the eerie appearance of the place.

Tommy Dowling was our leader, he also collected the halfpenny from each one of us weekly – this was to buy our candles by the packet, they cost more to buy in ones.

Tommy was the favourite story teller. His pale complexion and long face made him an ideal character, he also had very wispy blond hair and silver-framed glasses.

Some nights our trance would be broken by the voice of parents calling the kids for bed. Most of us were allowed to stay out very late – there was little danger in those days, the only fear we had was of ghosts. I could forget all the bad things about my home life and made the best of these special events.

I still laugh now as I recall one particular night during a story. Tommy had come to one line of his tale and uttered those immortal words, "If there is anybody up there, knock three times!"

As Tommy looked towards the ceiling there was a sudden tapping. Without speaking a word we all headed towards the stairway like bats out of hell; most of the candles had blown out and we were burned by the hot candle grease as we struggled to be first out. A quick exit was hampered by the fact that so many stairs were missing.

When we eventually gathered outside, convinced that some ghost had tried to make contact, no one wanted to leave each other to go our own separate way.

Suddenly our fear turned to hysterics as an old man appeared at the door. It was the sound of the one-legged man crossing his wooden floor that had put the fear of God into us. We had forgotten that Mr Hefferan above had a wooden leg.

There were many nights when we were told off for our laughing and yelling, as we would stand and talk planning our next meeting in the cellar. I would always hope that I would not have to play mother on the dates arranged.

It was never our intention to annoy or disturb anyone with our hilarity and we felt very put out when some people would open their windows and shout things, like "Go home you shower of little shites and get to bed." We would never answer back but moved on tittering about the night's events.

There are many people who would think that our preoccupation with ghost stories was strange, but we loved to scare ourselves silly. It was preferable to the other kind of fear I would often suffer at home. We only ever had good innocent fun and still to this day I enjoy a good old ghost story.

Danno and I would be so scared after some of our meetings that we used to hold on to each other as we entered the dark hallway to our house; unfortunately our hall light switch was at the furthest end of the hall. Danno sometimes did the dirty on me by pretending to wait outside the toilet for me and would lock himself in his room while I stood alone trying to pluck up the courage to flick the light off and run the few yards to the bedroom I shared with the rest of the family. I must admit there were times I would turn the light off when he was in the toilet and jump out on him in the dark; that got tiresome after he lashed out in the dark and nearly knocked my head off. These are the best memories of my life.

13

Our Favourite Sweet Shops

We certainly did not appear to have had the sweet shortage as bad as the children living in England.

We had shops scattered between houses all along our side of the street. Mahons' shop sold mainly groceries, though we mainly shopped there for broken biscuits. We were not too keen on the shopkeeper as it was he who would throw buckets of water on our chalk markings for our game of hopscotch.

Whites had to be our favourite, they had the finest display of assorted toffees and lollipops as well as liquorice pipes and sherbet dips. I will always remember that we could have ten honeybee caramels for one penny.

I recall how patient Mr White was as we walked up and down, over and over, before deciding what to spend our precious pennies on. He was a smart, distinguished looking man with a turned-up thick moustache and a silver watch on a chain in his waistcoat pocket.

His wife always wore a neat little pinny and her hair was always up in a little bun. She would look over the top of her little silver-framed spectacles and wring her hands, probably wishing we would hurry up. We could view her little sitting room from the shop counter and she would dust and polish in between serving. We were good loyal customers when we had money.

Uncle Dan would give us as much as two shillings each at the weekend. I have memories of choking myself by sucking sherbet too quickly through a straw.

The ultimate in pleasure was the bags of soft rock we bought from Plowmans' little shop in Tram Terrace.

My sweet tooth is as keen today as it was then.

The sweet tooth brings me back to when Danno and I were walking along Emmet road and witnessed Bolands' delivery van in collision with another vehicle, not what you'd expect then with so few vehicles on the roads.

I do not recall what type of vehicle it was, only that it stopped suddenly causing the Bolands' van trays of cakes to slide out of the back and on to the ground.

This was a dream come true. While the delivery man argued as to who was to blame, we helped ourselves to as many cream buns as we could; everybody knows that in those days cream was cream, and the jam was the best I have ever tasted. There were other people including adults who also helped themselves. Danno and I gave no thought to how much dirt we ate with the cakes straight off the road, we were hardy kids.

The memory of the van prompts me to tell you that as a toddler I was run over by one, it too was a delivery van for Haffners. Apparently the fact that in those days they were much higher off the ground saved my life. I had run in front of it and fallen over so the van was able to clear me as it went over my body. I must have been meant to be here.

Obviously I cannot elaborate on that event, with having no memory of it whatsoever. I only became aware of it when a passing nun from the nearby convent stopped and chatted with my mother and for some reason the nun had recalled the accident. I overheard the nun telling Mam about the sad day Mam had lost her little girl. Mam pointed towards me and said, "That's her beside me, Sister, she came through without a scratch."

I suppose that I can say life was more bearable without Dad at home. I remember on occasions when Bernie and I would stand and wave as Dad went back to base carrying his leave bag. Dad would kiss Bernie and swing her around and would then tell me to look after her till he came back. I was to wish many times that he never returned.

Most of my memories of Danno as a boy are of him coming and going and during the times Mam went off and left me in charge, he stayed well out of the way.

Looking after Leo was difficult as he was running about, but life was much harder after Sheila's arrival. Sheila was a very good child and cried little, but Leo had Bernie and I running around like a hare.

Mam had always made a point of telling me to stay indoors for the periods she went off with her friends. I used to be so pleased when it was only overnight. I hated it when it was over the whole weekend, life drags when you are young. It was all too much responsibility for a child of my age.

Looking back I would say that there were people watching out for us though it was never obvious, but food would appear from places with little said – that's the way the neighbours were. I suppose they may have spoken among themselves, there was never any outward show of hostility towards Mam for her neglect of us. Later in life I became aware that these people did not have a good word to say for Dad, but as young innocent children we could not have been told that our father was a philanderer and had many women both in Northern Ireland where he was stationed and much nearer home.

We would not have understood any of that, even though I had bumped into him myself out with women – to me as a child there was nothing wrong in that.

The Good Hearted People

I remember one special kind lady who lived in a little cottage within an area of Inchicore called 'The Puck'.

Her appearance blended well with the tiny neat home with clean shiny windows and white netting. She would very often come out and give me freshly made potato cakes or jammed scones as I sat on the piece of grass verge nearby waiting for other kids to come along and play. We never went hungry at home but other people always appeared to have more variety of food than we did. I have tried many times to recall that particular lady's name but it still escapes me.

Mrs Cummings was another nice neighbour, she had a daughter called Betty, who was about the same age as Bernadette – we had lots of her cast-off clothing, or should I say items she had outgrown. The nice thing was they never talked about what they gave us, there was never any fear that Betty would inform anyone of their generosity.

My closest friend was a girl called Angela. Her grandad was the local cobbler, he worked from his home, and my family were always given the first option of buying any unclaimed repaired shoes that people had not claimed within six months.

We never took shoes for repair, as we wore ours until they fell to bits. I would very often say that shoes fitted simply because they were sold off very cheaply even though they pinched badly, which is probably why today I have bunions like onions.

Dad's sister Molly made it clear when she visited us from England that she was embarrassed by our shabby attire, her son was immaculately dressed. Life in Britain was good for them. Auntie Molly had married a chap from a comfortably off family and Mam had always said she had become stuck-up.

On some occasions she brought adult clothing – some of her own and some from her sister, also living in Britain, and make clothes for Bernie and I on her machine in Gran's parlour. Dad's brother Mick would also contribute or perhaps it was Mary, Mick's wife – they lived near Molly in London. We were always very grateful for things received. I don't recall ever feeling inferior because we had less than others.

I have no memories whatsoever of life in Gran's house being occupied by anyone other than us. Apart from Dan, Bill and Paddy, Gran's family had all emigrated to England. The good thing about their visits, apart from seeing cousins, was the fact that Mam never went out and left us when they were in Ireland and they gave us money.

There was a pub on each end of our street, one near us on the corner of Emmet Road the other further up the road. We kids like to play outside the nearer of the two, we loved to peep in every time the door opened; we loved the smell of the beer-soaked sawdust that wafted out every time the door opened.

When Dad was home on leave he preferred the pub at the top of the road; we would never dare be seen anywhere near that one.

I can only recall the pub nearest us being called 'Buglars', though this has been disputed as of late. I think that it may have changed names and the people of my time carried on calling it by its previous name, that does happen as old habits die hard.

Though I had played outside the pub as a child, it was to be over forty-five years later before I set foot inside. I have to say pubs do not impress me in the slightest. I am pleased to say that there are more good memories of nice neighbours that I will always cherish – Lil Cleary, Mrs Reid and many more.

They probably will never have known just how grateful I was to have had them as neighbours.

Auntie Molly's Bloody Parcel

Although I loved the visits from our relatives from England, there is one I would rather forget.

Auntie Molly would have parcels redirected to our address, even though she was not staying at our address. One such parcel arrived one morning as Mam was going into the city and we were told that Molly would be over to pick it up.

Apart from the odd package of tea from Ceylon sent by Dad we did not usually receive parcels.

I am afraid that by the time Danno and I had finished prodding and poking and undoing a little bit of tape to try and nose, the package looked worse for wear. We still did not know what it contained. Molly lost little time on informing Mam and made remarks as to how badly mannered we were to do such a thing.

Mam hated Molly's haughty attitude and had become very angry. I did not get it too bad but Danno being the oldest got a very hard thrashing; we were usually very quick on our feet when Mam lost her temper but Mam appeared to hold on to Danno forever and I felt guilty because I did put most of the blame on him.

Uncle Paddy who had left with Molly and their son Christopher after Molly's outburst, returned for something they had left behind thus resulting in Mam easing up on Danno and letting him go.

Uncle Paddy told Mam the bloody parcel wasn't good enough reason to start a war and they would see us in a couple of days when everything had cooled down. Danno and I made our exit as Paddy was leaving.

I was feeling very sorry for Danno. I hated our Auntie at this moment, and Mam too for Danny's punishment. I hoped Molly would feel bad when she heard of Danno's punishment.

I would watch that night, as I had many times before, as

Mam would go to my sleeping brother's bed and gently say sorry as he slept. She would kiss him softly and say she would never do it again, she meant it, she always did! I remembered the punishment over the parcel every time I ever saw Auntie Molly. Why? You may say when it was Mam who punished for the deed. That simple, I loved our mam.

Looking back it is clear Mam needed help in many ways, but there was none available. There was nowhere to turn.

This account of our childhood cannot be put in any form of order, it is based on memories as they come.

Our Swimming Lesson From Dad

During one of Dad's leaves he decided it was time both Bernie and I should learn to swim. Mam had bought us both a pair of bloomers each, saying they would serve a dual purpose as a swimsuit and as normal knickers.

I can still see us now as we pulled on the large pink knickers which came to our knees, the elastic leaving ridges in our flesh. We were sure there was nothing to worry about as we set off on Dad's bicycle, Bernie sitting side saddle and me on the back carrier.

Dad had a framed lifesaving certificate hanging in the hall. He had apparently dived to the bottom of the canal during the search for a young boy who had fallen in. The story we heard many times was that Dad saved the boy, having first getting snagged up himself on some object at the bottom of the canal.

I put away the memory of the rescue I had seen myself on another occasion when a boy drowned. Our dad was a lifesaver, nothing could go wrong – could it?

My bottom hurt as Dad cycled over humps along the canal bank, and at one stage I fell off. I shouted after him and watched as he lowered one foot to the earth and waited for me to jump on again.

I was sure that for our first few lessons Dad would use the small stream that ran along just a few yards away. It was a great shock to be thrown straight into the canal yards from the lock. I was petrified as Bernie appeared to drift in the opposite direction to me and felt the weight of the water that had weighted the leg of my bloomers pull me down.

I have no idea as to how many times I went under but know I saw vegetation and rubbish on the canal bed. I was utterly convinced that if it came to a choice of saving only one of us, that I would be the one to perish. I usually prayed when frightened, but could not bring myself to utter a word each time I surfaced.

My next clear memory was Dad shoving me on to the embankment and a man with a bicycle shouting abuse at Dad as he carried on swimming. The man told Dad what a cruel bastard he was and that he wasn't fit to have children.

Bernie was huddled up close to me with the only towel we had wrapped around our shoulders.

I recall Dad telling the shouting man to stay where he was until he got out of the water, but thank God the man jumped on the cycle and rode off.

The least Dad would have done was throw the man into the canal so we were glad he had ridden away, we were not fit to take any more fear.

Dad assured us that we would improve with time. I was just happy to be alive. Thank heavens Dad never found the time to carry on the lessons. It was fifty years before my sister and I lost our fear of water, thanks to Dad.

Playing With Fire

I think it can be safely said that Mam's priorities were not in her children's favour.

Most children were in danger during play or recreation of one kind or another but we were at risk more than most. Other kids usually had someone to run home to every day, we were not so lucky, though I think that somebody up there was looking over us.

I remember one morning waking to a lot of talk and commotion going on outside, and after listening to neighbours learned that a family of five children had lost their lives in a house fire. The house in Kilmainham was not very far from us so I tried to join the onlookers who had been prevented from going past a cordon at the bottom of the road.

The whole area was thick with the smell of burning. Mam managed to find me and took me back home, and as usual with that sort of tragedy people made comments to each other, like 'Where were the parents?' By the end of the day the place was alive with rumour. I can recall thinking that it could easily have been us. There were many nights I was at risk of such a thing occurring. I was woken many times by Sheila and Leo as babies wanting a hot drink in the middle of the night and did what I had seen Mam do often. I would make a little mound of the fire embers and throw paraffin over them to set them alight. I would then heat the milk in a saucepan above the flames, adding more fuel as the flame dimmed.

My reason for this dangerous habit was simply so as not to have to unlock the bedroom door and go upstairs in the middle of the night – no doubt spooked by too many ghost stories.

Another dangerous pastime as a child was playing along the canal bank, especially around the locks. We did this whether Mam was at home or away, it was great fun. The men who took the Guinness barges would allow us to get on from one lock to another as a reward for opening and closing the lock gates. If I had the smaller kids with me Bernie would run along the side with the two of them in the pram while I had my turn, and then I would do the same while she boarded the barge and had her go.

Little did Mam ever know how near the edge we lived as we ran along the bumpy banks and on the rare occasion tipping the pram over with our haste to try and beat the boat not to mention that the baby strap was not always on and we very often almost tipped the pram into the canal! I must say that the couple of near misses did make me more careful but, to be honest, I was not really old enough for so much responsibility.

Mam certainly put herself first, she was very irresponsible and I will never know how she could ever justify her neglect towards us. I will never know if she took time to reflect on what she deprived us of. I do resent the theft of my precious time. I know I cannot have it back but it helps me to punish Mam by saying it – this is my way, I am telling it as seen through my eyes only.

The Funny Nice People Of Vincents Street

The Delahuntes were two lovely people, they were brother and sister. I do not recall their parents, they may have been orphans. May was the older one and took care of Guck – no idea what that was short for.

Although Guck did play normal games like football and hurling, he had a special liking for his hoop or plain old bicycle wheel. He really believed that by taking it with him when he went for the messages for his sister that it got him back quicker. I would not argue with that – my own brother also got back twice as quick if he met Guck on the way back. No one ever walked alongside Guck, if you wanted to chat to him you had to keep up as he hit the wheel with one hand and clasped the messages with the other, it was indeed a great mode of transport.

Rachel Boswell was a gypsy girl whose caravan was parked permanently in a corner of 'The Puck' which was situated near 'Tram Terrace' – these places were all in or around my street. Rachel taught me to make paper flowers in her lovely caravan. The rest of the family would be away most of the day selling the many wares the family made to make a living. She showed me how to cut tin cans, crimping the thinly cut tin and make ornamental miniature trees; this was made effective by squeezing the tip of each thin strip of crimped tin around a tiny piece of shaped coloured paper, giving the effect of leaves. Her family's caravan was one of four that had been there for as long as I could remember.

Two of the other nice folk were Mr and Mrs Daly – that's what we called them, though people liked to point out that the lady was only a 'housekeeper' and that they were not wed. How silly of anyone to think it mattered to us.

Mr Daly was always afforded the full name but his lady was May to me and most other folk. She was a lovely, kind, friendly human being and was very fond of me and I of her.

I remember the first time May invited me into her orchard. The house was only a stone's throw from 'Cragans House' and the famous spooky cellar.

The sight before my eyes could only be described as fairyland, compared to my own concrete backyard it was magical. Though May had told me to help myself to the many fruits from the trees, it was not my first consideration. I just wanted to walk around and take in the splendour of the garden.

Mr Daly was a very nice gentleman, but preferred the peace and quiet of his own surroundings, which is why May could only invite me in while he was at work.

May loved people and children. I like to think that I was special to her, perhaps the child she never had; she was quite ancient in my young eyes – maybe about forty!

Other people who come to mind were the Clearys who lived next door to the nearest pub. Jimmy lived with an aunt and his granny.

Marie O'Neill and her older sister Carmel lived with their parents though the image of the father's face has now faded; we played with the younger girl, Marie – a bit stuck-up but nice with it. I remember she hated it when it was her turn to turn the skipping rope; she was very clever at playing the piano though.

Another family were the Kinsellas. We played with the younger girl whose name was Etna. She had a bigger brother, Peter. Our nickname for him was 'leather arse'. He walked just like John Wayne and that was what we kids called John Wayne.

Our good friend Betty Cummings was a nice girl but had bad mood swings, this was a nuisance as she usually owned everything we played with and every time she sulked she took her things home.

Andy The Ambulance Man

There was a time when it was quite acceptable to chastise other people's children with a smack across the face or a kick up the backside, though most children never admitted to their parents that they had earned one. It was not something kids in those days bragged about. My mother was no exception to the rule and had on many an occasion chastised another child for bad behaviour, though not as often as she belted us.

The strange thing about Mam was that even though she battered us and accepted that maybe other people would also give us a wallop, it made a difference if Mam did not like the person who gave us the thumping! There was one such occasion...

There was a place called 'Bryans Yard', it had four houses on each side. In one of those houses lived our ambulance man and in another was a family called Gough. For some reason my mum disliked Mrs Gough quite strongly. My brother Danny had a fight with one of Mrs Gough's sons resulting in the lady hitting my brother. Now we were not usually in the habit of expecting back-up from parents but mischief overtook me and I lost no time in informing Mam about her old enemy.

Mam's knock on Mrs Gough's door nearly woke the dead and before too many words were spoken the tall lady shoved my short mum. It was not long before the two women were on the ground, pulling hair and name calling.

Mam was not doing badly for her size when Andy the ambulance man arrived and parted the two women. Normally the person responsible for breaking up fights would have been booed, but this was our hero, so we accepted the end to our amusement.

Andy was a hero who was there for us on numerous occasions. One of the times that comes to mind was when a lad who was passing through our area began to cough and choke, he fell to his knees and turned a funny colour.

Andy soon arrived and got to work on the lad; when thumping his back did not do the trick Andy grabbed him in a sort of bear hug until suddenly the cause of the problem popped out of the boy's mouth. We all breathed a sigh of relief to see the shiny marble roll on the ground. The boy cried loudly, it was probably more from relief than anything.

I would say that apart from the rescue of the drowning boy that this was one of the most dramatic rescues we had witnessed in our area. Usually when kids from other areas strayed on other kids' streets they were questioned and chased off, but for that stranger we were full of concern.

Andy came to the rescue again for us on the day my little brother needed hospital treatment for a burned bottom. Mam had removed the top of the range and placed it on the stone tiles below while she put more fuel in the fire. While Mam's head was turned Leo had decided to sit on the range cover. His flesh was still on the cover after Mam removed him from it and he was screaming unmercifully.

As was usual when any member of my family was in pain, I too suffered with him, and ran for Andy who took us to the emergency department of St. Stevens hospital.

After seeing that we were being attended to, Andy left Mam, myself and Leo and returned home. Mam soon ran out of patience and returned home also, leaving me to fetch Leo home by myself.

I felt very distressed as I sat outside the dressing room listening to my little brother cry as the nurses dressed his wound, it seemed to take forever. I requested that I come and hold his hand to reassure him and became very upset when one of the nurses tapped him on the legs for not keeping still. I could hold back no longer and became cheeky telling the nurse that I would hit her should she slap my brother again.

I noticed how dirty my brother's feet were. He was in the habit of running around barefoot, his hands were also grubby but mine were not much better.

The nursing staff were none too happy that Mam had disappeared and questioned my ability at taking Leo home. Mam had not left me any money for the bus and Leo needed carrying, face down. I was about to break out in tears when a voice asked if he could assist, he was going to upper Inchicore and had transport outside. I readily accepted and was soon sitting on the back of the man's dray, Leo spread face down across my lap.

I enjoyed the clip clop sound of his horse and the sympathetic looks we received from people seeing Leo's predicament. Mam was amused at our mode of transport and thanked the man for bringing us home.

Leo was glad to be back home and looked pitiful lying face down on Mam's double bed. Clean lines were made on his dirty face from the many tears he had shed. The wild wee boy had his activities drastically curtailed for some weeks to come.

People in our area were quite used to seeing me pounding the streets for Leo, he was a wiry little wanderer and most of the shopkeepers on the main Emmet road would hold on to him if they spotted him, they knew I would soon be there asking if anyone saw him. Leo was such a free spirit that I don't think he would have survived if the traffic had been heavy in those days.

Leo's welfare was the biggest worry of my young life, I had always worried about him.

On the rare occasions I attended school, my mind was preoccupied with him. I do not recall any other child of my age with so much responsibility, though it did become the norm in my life.

I recall coming home from school on another occasion and seeing Leo lying on Mam's bed. I ran straight to him and saw that he was very pale and had his face resting on a folded nappy. Mam explained that he had again attended the casualty department in St. Steven's hospital.

I had shown Leo how to draw and would sit him at the table with pencil and paper to occupy him, and it was while doing this that the accident happened. Mam said that one minute he was sitting dangling his legs and scribbling and in seconds he was screaming and covered in blood. It appeared he tilted the chair and slipped, causing the sharp pencil to penetrate the roof of his mouth.

The doctors said that he would be sore for some time but there was little else they could do, that Mam was to take him back if the bleeding continued too long.

I felt so sorry for the poor little fellow as he lay there with the blood-stained nappy and dried blood on his little face. At first I thought that Mam had lost her temper with him and beat him, though the smaller ones usually escaped smacks.

His recovery took some time and he lost weight in the weeks to follow. Wild as he was, I still preferred to see him back to being his mischievous little self again.

I am a firm believer in children learning how to take responsibility but not to the degree where they lose their childhood, no one should take that away.

During my travel to the local police station in Kilmainham which is where I would head for when Leo disappeared for long periods I would take my mind off my worries by taking in the pleasures of my journey on foot.

I popped into the grotto of St. Michael's Chapel and lit a candle in front of The Blessed Virgin asking her to help me find my brother. I would always put a penny in for the candle if I had one, failing that I would promise to pay double next time.

I would then go across the road to where I knew someone would chase me for walking down their lane, I enjoyed proving to myself that they would never catch me. They were strange kids who lived in the little houses, though most kids had a thing about their own patch. Jimmy Cafferty was the only boy I knew by name.

I would again cross back over the road and stand gazing in the window of a shop called 'The Coombe Dairy'. It was the only creamery shop around. I stood fascinated as the ladies weighed out the butter, slapping it between the wooden spatulas.

In those days people could buy butter by the ounce. I loved salty butter and watching the cheese being cut with wire also gave me a thrill. I don't know why Mam never bought hard cheese; we did occasionally have processed.

It may appear odd that I would be on my way to look for my lost brother, but I never had any fear that anything dreadful would happen. I always knew he would be found, that's the way it was then. The last stop before the police station was the most exciting. I would stand looking through the famous Kilmainham jail which we were told housed political prisoners who had opposed British rule in Ireland. I had little or no interest in its history, my interest was much more that that.

The historians' versions of what took place there within the walls of Kilmainham jail was not half as interesting as the ghost stories told by local people. You have to remember that we were poor kids trying hard to survive the poverty and neglect from our own folk, we had no interest in tales of something which seemed far removed from our lives.

There were many stories of ghosts that walked the grounds of the jail. I would never look towards the building if I passed by after dark, mainly because stories of ghosts usually refer to night. As a child I remember the place was always locked with thick chains and big black locks.

I also remember the greeting I used to get from the guards as I would eventually enter the police station to see if anyone had brought my lost brother in. I would be answered before I even asked the question. "No darlin', we haven't got your brother." Usually Leo would have been found by the time I arrived home. There was never a time where he was gone for the whole day, and I could never get really angry with the little terror for the worry he caused – most times I just wanted to cuddle him though he was not the sort of toddler who allowed a lot of cuddling, unlike his baby sister Sheila, she would let you fuss her forever.

Of Course There Were Good Days

We were not the poorest kids in the neighbourhood and looking back now can say that, had Mam been a better manager of money we could have had a much better upbringing, after all the pay allowance from the Airforce was probably better than some jobs paid.

Mam would take advantage of the cheap food sold to the poor of the local people; it was cooked and sold from the kitchen of the High School in Tram Terrace. Bernie and I would take our containers and have them filled up with stew and milk pudding. I loved semolina. We got quite a lot of both for sixpence.

We bigger kids usually earned our Sunday matinee money

either by knocking on doors and asking could we have leftover food for the pig lady – she would pay us judging by how much we had in the collecting bucket.

It was harder earning it working for the local shop. When the log or turf lorry made a delivery, it would be dropped off on the road outside the shop and we would earn a shilling for the best part of the day – the trouble with that job was that it was not regular.

I was usually the only girl who did that job. I was very much a tomboy. That brings me to the memory of a day I was allowed to play cowboys and Indians with the boys, some had home-made wooden guns and those of us who didn't pointed two fingers and pretended.

The biggest embarrassment was the indignity of being 'shot', so I tried proving I could do anything they could to avoid being captured and shot – so I climbed a tree. I was struggling very hard when I heard laughter from the boys and suddenly realised I was not wearing knickers. That was to be the last time I would try climbing knickerless. The embarrassment was painful.

It was quite common in those days for kids to fall over and expose a bare bottom; it was commonplace to hear jeering boys calling someone 'bare arse'.

The memory of not having many changes of clothing up-sets me now, but there were thousands in the same boat. I re-member that Mam would only wash when the washing was piled high and that could result in every stitch of clothing you pos-sessed (apart from what you were wearing) being in the wash pile, and with no mangle they could take a week to dry.

Twice yearly or so, Mam would get a lump sum allowance to spend on clothing, but knickers was never on Mam's list of pri-orities. Cardigans, socks and sandals plus the odd dress, and on one very special occasion Bernie and I had a brand new coat. I can still see them now – Bernie's was blue and navy tweed with matching navy velvet on the collar, pockets and a half belt, mine was a boyish double-breasted beige and brown tweed. I do not recall wearing it very often – it spent most of the time in James Street Pawn Brokers as did Bernie's, and I would say that I only ever had a couple of times' wear from it before it was passed down to Bernie. She had as little wear from it as I did, not that she minded, she thought my coat was too boyish.

I am glad to say that these kinds of memories can now cause me to smile. If lack of clothing, tatty or otherwise was the only hardship we had endured, we would have been happy children.

Our Own Slippery Slope

Going back to our own forms of entertainment reminds me of our favourite winter enjoyment. Today we would have said it was our very own piste.

The sloping lane ran down behind the back of our backyard. As you looked down the lane there were two entrances – one either side that led to the yards used for the buses, the one on the right went right to the wall that divided our backyard from it. This side was used mainly for the old seats and tyres and the few old buses no longer in use. We often fished up some of the old broken wood on a hook attached to a rope.

It was hard work ripping the wood away from the upholstery as the seats had been well put together in those days. We would break some of the wood, tie it in little bundles and sell to the local people for a halfpenny a bundle, this was another way of earning money for our Sunday picture matinees.

The slippery slope was our favourite place after snow fell in winter. We would find whatever we could use as a sledge and enjoy the feeling of freedom as we sped down the slope and walked up to the top again and repeated the exercise over and over.

We were a nuisance to the bus drivers who wanted access to the bus yards, and very often the yardman would throw substances on our glass-like surface to deter us from using the lane as a ski slope.

For the few of us who could stay out late at night after the yard was closed it was very enjoyable.

I remember using old tin basins with old rags inside to save our bottoms when holes appeared. The later we were out the colder it was, but we enjoyed every painful minute.

We never considered for one moment that we were making the surface a danger to other people wanting to use the lane. We never set out deliberately to cause any problems; we were not bad, just playful kids having fun.

Looking back now it is easy to see the danger in everything, not only to others but also ourselves, because the lane we slid down went straight on to the main Emmet road. Once our basins or whatever we used for our sled picked up speed there was no stopping.

We were probably classed as little pests, but kids like us were only taking fun and enjoyment wherever we could get it free.

The Gum Chewing Man In Uniform

It never occurred to us as children to question why our parents showed us so little affection, but I don't suppose we could really make comparisons. We did have some fun days with Mam, but it was always dampened by her asking me to do things I really hated doing – things like having to go to our local shop and ask for credit. I found it embarrassing when other customers were behind me.

The other infuriating thing would be when she would suddenly inform me in the evening that she was going to the pictures and I would have to stay in and mind the house and younger ones.

It was on such an occasion that I decided to disobey and take the little ones out with me and go and play hopscotch on our favourite corner. I had waited until Mam had disappeared around the corner and gave her enough time to have got on the local bus in town.

Bernie took turns at watching the little ones while I participated in the game. We had been enjoying ourselves for some time when I became aware of a familiar laugh and male and female chatter. I became conscious of our friends staring with mouths agape and was astounded to see Mam come towards us with a young man in uniform. It was too late to run, so we stood aside as the two walked past. Mam did not say a word though

31

the other kids said hello to her and the uniformed man asked us all if we would like some chewing gum.

I was still dumbstruck and was even too much in awe of the man's accent even to worry about the fact that Mam might kill me for disobeying her and taking the children out. The man spoke the same as the men in the cowboy movies. I wondered how she got to know a cowboy.

I took the wee ones home and Bernie helped me with the kids, like heating a drink and getting them settled down for the night, at least that had been the intention initially but not before curiosity had got the better of us and we had followed Mam at a safe distance. We had followed just far enough to satisfy ourselves that she and her friend had gone to the local cinema. We felt better knowing that she was not far, just a stone's throw away.

Bernie and I lay awake, chatting in whispers as we usually did after we got the little ones settled for the night. We felt more secure after Danny would let the catch off the front door; we would read comics too, but threw them on the floor as soon as Mam's key turned in the lock, and pretend to be asleep.

There was no chance Mam would wake me to tell me off for my disobedience, for fear of disturbing the little ones. There was never any mention the following day either, so I though it best to forget about enquiring about the cowboy with the gum.

As I have said before, sometimes Mam could be so funny and amusing, childlike even, but even on her bad days after a belting I could always find it easy to forgive her. Forgiveness towards Dad would never come easy. I felt the pain each time Dad beat Mam – the memories haunt me.

I recall a night when I woke to see Dad interrogate Mam as he pushed her on to the small chair behind the bedroom door; the bedroom light was not on but the hall light shone through the half open door, he slapped her face as he had hold of her hair and the next day I saw the splattered blood on the wallpaper.

Whatever wrongs Mam may have done in Dad's eyes, nothing will ever convince me that she ever deserved such punishment, no one does.

Mam's bruises may have faded in time but the mental scars Dad inflicted will never fade, the beatings I only heard from another room were equally as upsetting as those I witnessed close up.

Mam's Snobbery

As children growing up in Inchicore, the word 'snob' was not even part of our vocabulary and we were certainly not in any position to look down on anybody, so I still laugh to myself when I recall some of Mam's commands.

She would warn us to stay out of certain areas and tell us not to mix with certain kids; 'Keogh Square' was one such place, it had been an Army Barracks that was used for many of Dublin's homeless or people waiting for Corporation Houses. There were some very nice people there, I went to school with three girls from the 'Barracks' as it was known by the locals.

I will admit that some of the kids who lived there were very territorial and would belt strangers with stones, but in reality, our street was only separated from it by the high stone wall that went from one end of Vincent Street to the other. I do not remember the names of the three girls that I went to school with and played with in the playground, but two were sisters – their surname was Coleman and I had been to their house many times. Stones were never thrown at me while I was in their company.

Mam was always happy to let us attend the birthday parties of the 'better off' kids – some of them had given us their hand down clothing, but I can honestly say that none of those kids ever reminded me or my sister that we were wearing their 'hand-me-downs'. They may have appeared to be toffee-nosed, but they were nice.

We never ever had birthday celebrations in our house, we were made aware of the day but I do not recall presents, to be perfectly honest I cannot say that it mattered.

Mam had little time for answering our questions nor did she take a lot of notice of much of what we did.

I clearly remember an occasion when Mam was busy doing the Monday wash, it usually took a whole day. I cannot recall which of the two smallest children was sitting in the pram by the window in the top kitchen, I think it was Leo. Anyway, I became interested in the attempted rescue of a horse that had become stuck in the mud near the 'Mac' river.

I watched the group of men pull at the rope that was tied around the animal and every now and then I ran home to let Mam know how the rescue was progressing. I did not appreciate how uninteresting it was to Mum as she struggled with the washboard and the load of washing. I do remember how red Mam's face was and still see the sweat wetting her hair.

I did help by seeing to the baby and standing on a chair in the yard below to put the odd thing on the line, but found the animal rescue much more exciting and carried on relaying the latest happenings to Mam.

After what seemed like a lifetime, the men had to seek the aid of a man with a mechanical hoist until finally the horse was saved – or so I thought!

Mam told me that the horse had probably escaped from the slaughter house and that it would probably still finish up being slaughtered. I suppose that there was little time back then for sentiment. I realise now that Mam herself had grown up with cold parents. I do not mean that in a nasty way, but Mam's dad was an old grump and Granny was a very serious woman, no one used words of endearment.

The Bad Winter And My Friend Angela

It was the winter of 1947, I was nine years old and was sent into town to do some errands for Mam.

After going around some of the roadside stalls, I walked along towards James Street Pawn shop to retrieve Uncle Dan's best trousers – they went in every Monday and came back out again every Friday, like clockwork.

It was snowing quite heavily as I got off the number 21 bus just past St. Michael's Church in Emmet Road. My last errand

34

should have been at Bolands Bakers on the opposite side of the road, but as I got off the bus I dropped half a crown in the snow. My fingers had numbed and as I tried to swap the shopping from one hand to the other, the coin slipped from my cold hand.

I was dressed rather inadequately for the weather and my brain also seemed numb as I felt around in the snow for the lost coin, some people tried helping me as I became more frantic but most were keen to get home out of the terrible weather. I eventually had to give up and went home without the bread from the bakery and the lost coin.

I hoped my pitiful appearance would melt Mam's stare as I tried explaining but she lashed out angrily at me, and by the time she was finished I was much warmer. I made straight for the door once she loosened her grip on me and headed where I usually did on these occasions – to my friend Angela.

She lived with her parents in a little old whitewashed cottage off Tram Terrace. I was always welcome there and would receive either a mug of sweet cocoa or tea and bread and dripping.

I poured my heart out to her, calling Mam all sorts of names and saying how much I hated her; this was the usual pattern, she knew I loved my mum. Once my cardigan sleeve was saturated from the tears and nose-wiping, I would be happy again until the next time.

Angela was always there for me and even if we had fallen out beforehand my appearance with tear-filled eyes always broke the ice. I too would always be there for her especially on a couple of sad occasions when her mum had lost very young babies soon after birth – we would pray together and go to St. Michael's and light candles.

It was normal practice back then to have the open coffin at home prior to the burial of deceased relatives and I remember those occasions as Angela's mum's babies lay in their kitchen-cum-dining room.

Angela and I would continually touch the tiny hands of the babes and rearrange the little rosary beads that were wrapped around the dead babies' hands. It never seemed right that we would have to put such little souls into the ground for burial.

I recall the time when Angela was told to set the table for dinner and as she lifted the tiny coffin, she looked all around for an empty space and finally chose the draining board by the sink. It all seemed so natural to her, even though one of the babies had died as the result of her mum falling asleep in bed while breast feeding – apparently the baby suffocated.

The Move And Betsy's Birth

The actual move from Inchicore to Ballyfermot is almost a total blank, apart from the odd memory of pushing some of our belongings along in the old brown pram and that Mam was with me on a couple of the trips and I have absolutely no recall of my baby sister's arrival soon after we moved in.

It may have been that I was too busy trying to get to know other kids and spent time exploring the vast housing estate that seemed to go on forever, or perhaps I found the move so traumatic that I erased it from my mind. I do know that I still returned to play with my friends in Vincent Street and would still visit our old house which our Uncle Dan carried on renting – he carried on living there even though other people moved in and took tenancy of what was our part of the house.

I do know that Mam never again went out and left me in charge after the move. It could explain why I had never formed the same maternal bond with Betsy as I had with Leo and Sheila, though I would say that my maternal feelings with Leo were the stronger – he had been a difficult little chap to cope with after Sheila was born, but she was a very good child, you could almost forget she was in the house. I suppose only a psychologist could explain the 'whys' and so on!

I hated the vastness of Ballyfermot or 'Bally Far Off' as it became known. The new house had a bathroom with a proper bath – that meant little to me, there was no comparison at bathing in the real bath with tepid water and the wonderful comfort of the tin bath in front of the fire and the warm towels that had been warmed on the stool by the fire.

As if having to make new friends wasn't hard enough we then had to change schools. We opted to join the large number of other kids on the estate who went on the free bus to a school in town – it was called Whitefriars St. School We would sing every morning as we rode along – it had obviously been made up by the local kids and went something like this:

"Whitefriars Street School, is a very nice school,
it's made of sticks and plaster,
The only thing that's wrong with it,
is the baldy headed Masters."

If there were more words I don't remember them and have no memories of any particular teachers. I know I found it difficult to try and keep up with other kids, we had missed quite a lot of schooling.

Dad's Demob

I do not recall having known in advance that Dad was coming out of the Airforce for good, and had very mixed feelings about the prospects of what kind of change it would make in our lives. There had been a long gap between his last leave and his demob which I have to say was heavenly peaceful, though I had heard during my eavesdropping that Dad now had a 'Mot' in Northern Ireland – in today's language it meant he had a woman friend; that kind of talk was not permitted among children and Mam never discussed these sorts of things with her children. I had heard that Dad had many such relationships while in Inchicore but I was too young to understand the significance of such rumours.

Life did change quite dramatically and Dad got a job in the local Railway workshop only a stone's throw from our back garden wall. We could stand on the railing at the end of our garden and look into the window of the signalman's room and Dad's workplace was only on the other side of the track. We children often chatted to the signalman through the window – we never told him our dad worked there, in case he told Dad and we would be told off for standing on the fence.

It took some time to get used to the noise of the trains, but we eventually slept through it. I remember that those of us nearest the signal box had the dirtiest washing – the steam was often filthy. I do remember that our immediate neighbours were lovely people and we got on very well with them.

Life seemed almost normal for a short time and Dad even took Mam into town to shop with the lump sum he received from the Air Force. Bernie and myself were bought our first ever pair of fur-lined boots and a pair of wellingtons each. We also had the extra treat of a new velvet dress each – Bernie's was pink with white lace collar and cuffs and mine was dark blue. Treats were very rare, even at Christmas we received the same things year after year. Don't get me wrong, I was not ungrateful, I appreciated everything, but these were the most exquisite clothes we had ever owned.

It was not long before tension started to build up. Dad had made the local pub, 'The Old Pine Tree', his regular and his visits to it were regular!

On my way to and from the local park, I would very often spot Dad behaving very friendly with other women, and even spotted him arguing with one and then smack her hard across her face with the back of his hand – blood spilled from her nose.

I kept my silence about what I had witnessed and got a closer look at the lady some days later as she headed towards the pub. She had two front teeth missing. Dad was not aware that I had ever seen him and I am also ashamed to admit that as long as it was someone else and not my mam who was taking beatings it did not matter, after all Mam had to live with him, these women did not.

Rows began to take place between my parents and I began to notice a pattern of behaviour. It was usual to be told to go upstairs when they were rowing – it always sounded like an interrogation, then the silences during meals; it was also a sign that Mam was going to get a hiding before the night was over.

I began to live with my stomach permanently knotted as

any civility between my parents dwindled. I had never mentioned the events I had seen between my father and the woman and Dad had never taken Mam out with him to the pub, though to be honest she had little interest in pubs and apart from going to the shops or town, she had not been out anywhere since we left Inchicore nearly a year before. My mother eventually sought the help of a local priest; he came to our house and tried talking to Dad – that was a mistake, he opened our front door and told the priest to f..k off. That sort of language, especially directed towards the clergy, was disgraceful and was not acceptable back then.

Dad had obviously taken over control of money matters now, Mam seemed to be finding it much more difficult to manage. Mam was never the world's best manager, but we never went hungry; however, the cupboards were more bare since Dad took over and he made no provision for the various necessary household items that everyone needs, especially having just moved into newer housing. Perhaps Dad needed the money to treat his friends in the pub.

The rows between our parents increased, most of them started in the bedroom, which is where most of the others through their lives had done.

I had long been aware that Mam had always tried not to cry out when she was being beaten, she had always tried to keep that to herself, but I could see her flinch as she tried to comb her hair and could always tell that her head had been punched or banged against the wall. Mam's hair was thick and wiry, auburn in colour and sometimes it hurt so much to comb after a beating, she just saturated it with water. It used to look terrible.

It seems ironic, looking back, that Dad began to tell me how to fight for myself and never allow boys to get away with hitting me. He taught me to spar up with my fists. The opportunity arose one day when a boy of my own age tried taking a turn on the swing I had erected on the lamp post outside my front door. I argued first and tried to warn the boy off, then suddenly found myself acting on Dad's training and before I knew it I had punched the boy on the nose causing it to bleed badly. It went against the kind of kid I was. I became scared and ran inside, I was really upset and Dad's praise for what I had just done did not help.

It was strange that his only show of affection towards me was for punching someone. Dad had never inflicted beatings on his children. We were obedient on one word of command from him, in fact Mam had always been the one who gave us older ones the pastings, but she was always tender towards the little ones.

I have to say that I tried very hard not to go around hitting people after the boy who tried to have a go on my swing, in fact I tried hard at talking my way out of trouble and rows. The boy's nose had been broken, but we became friends later though not before he had come to my front door and kicked in one of the door panels.

Mam Dares To Talk Back

It came as quite a shock to come in from play one evening and hear Mam accusing Dad of womanising. She had dared to confront him and I appeared at the moment that Mam had thrown the photo of a dark-haired woman on the floor in front of him. I was immediately ordered upstairs and took the other kids with me – I never did find out what had happened before I came in, but was sure Mam would pay dearly for it.

I recall being downstairs with Mam and the children and a deathly silence as Dad shaved in front of the kitchen sink in our kitchen-dinette. I did not have to guess where Dad was going and what Mam would have coming when night came.

I recall Mam picking the baby up and going upstairs. My father followed her and another exchange of words could be heard down below.

After a short silence there was a thud on the floor above and Mam and the baby screamed together. I could do nothing but sit numb in the chair, almost strangled by Leo and Sheila. The younger ones always came very close for reassurance when the rows started.

Within minutes Dad disappeared out the front door and Mam came down holding the whimpering baby. I watched Mam run across the road to a close neighbour and on return she told us that she had to leave before Dad came home that night. Mam cried and said she had no idea where she was going, but she would visit us when she was settled, stating that it would be within the hours that Dad was working.

We had done all of our crying before Dad got home that night. Danno and I were the only two still awake, the other three were fast asleep through Bernie turned quite often and was still fretfully sighing in her sleep.

Dad showed no kind of emotion on hearing Mam had left but assured us that we would be much better off without her. He called her some nasty names. How I wished I could find the courage to tell him just how much we would miss her and how we would be waiting patiently for her first visit. We always kept our tears for times when Dad was not around.

Life Without Mam Was Lonely

The weeks that followed were miserable, made worse by Dad sitting us down regularly and questioning us about Mam's movements while he was in the forces. We went along with everything he said, even when he put words in our mouths, it made life more bearable.

I used to look out of the bus window on the way to and from school in the hope of seeing Mam and on numerous occasions thought I did. Dad had become harder on Danno – perhaps he thought that my brother was lying when he told Dad he could not remember things during questioning, but Danno never did take note of anything. He had always enjoyed his freedom and play and was not aware of most of what went on at home.

As promised, Mam did make contact with us via her friend who lived opposite; the visits were on Saturdays while Dad was working.

Dad did eventually discover our secret and stayed at home one Saturday and waited to see if Mam would attempt to come to us as we did not go to her as was arranged. She did not come to our door but as she left her friend's house and walked up the road on the way to the bus stop Dad sent me over to call her some names. I did not at the time know what they meant but Mam's expression spoke volumes. Mam handed me a brown paper bag and told me the content was for me and that she would see us next week. The bag contained a skirt she had made for me by cutting down one of her own.

I cried my heart out because we missed the visit, but cried many times in later life when I found out the meaning of the nasty message I had delivered on the orders of my father.

On Mam's next visit all of us except Danno left with Mam. We were all living in a tiny cottage that Mam and her friend Jim had set up home in. It was cramped, but I was happy to be with Mam.

We had never known anyone who had spent time in an institution but the rumours were bad enough to terrify, so the odd snippets I picked up between Jim and Mam gave me reason to believe that Mam was very fearful that we could end up in one.

I took the children out as often as possible to give them freedom from our very cramped living space. It was while we played in the lane near the cottage one Saturday that I spotted Dad enter the lane on a cycle. I immediately ushered the family inside and locked the door, warning Mam that Dad was outside.

Mum took hold of the baby and Bernie held Sheila while I held tightly on to Leo and tried to make the situation a game by telling him to hush, that Mary Holly was outside – it was something that Mam used to say to us when she wanted us to come in when it was getting dark. I do not know who Mary Holly was supposed to be, but it worked in keeping the kids quiet while Dad ranted outside the door and we pretended to be out.

We found it funny to hear Dad try and speak in a country accent by repeating "hello, is there anyone at home?" It was hard keeping the smaller ones still and the ranting seemed to go on forever. Dad knew we were there and when he received no reaction he became angry and called to each of us by name, informing us that we were going to court and would probably be put away.

I became very scared after he cycled away and begged Mam to save us. It had not helped Mam that Dad had yelled through the door that if we were put away to remember that it would be all Mam's fault. I am ashamed to admit it but I literally begged Mam to return to Dad, really believing that all could be well. I was too young and innocent to realise that I was asking Mam to risk her life to save us.

Mam and Jim talked a lot that evening and we were all on our way back to Dublin the following day.

Our arrival back home is sketchy except for the shouting that took place and the memory of Dad trying to push Mam out of the window. I believe my guilt for asking Mam to return has caused me to blank things out, but Mam was gone again with the smaller children.

I recall Dad persuading me to go into Goldenbridge Orphanage on a voluntary basis, that it would persuade the Judge who would eventually make a decision during my parents' separation hearing to place us all together in Goldenbridge.

Dad made the idea sound good, after all, it was on the old street in Inchicore where I used to live and the orphan girls who used to speak to us seemed happy enough! I was not to know that the freedom was for those with special privileges.

I cannot recall how much time elapsed before I was allowed home for a Sunday visit but, when evening came and it was time to go back, I locked myself in the bathroom and refused to go back.

I was not aware if the nuns had informed Dad that I had already tried escaping from Goldenbridge by trying to squeeze through the main gates, which were kept locked.

The new woman in Dad's life was at our house that day, (I don't think she had actually moved in at this time) but she persuaded Dad not to force me to return.

I suppose I was too young and scared to look at things as logically as Dad had pointed out about how my behaviour would be taken into account by the Judge in Court, such as my attempt at escape. The dreaded day for the hearing came, but the journey there is a blank.

The Day Of The Court Hearing

The well-polished wooden benches and the amount of people wearing black gave the feeling of being in a funeral parlour. I suppose at that time, I felt it was the end of our lives.

I cannot recall what was said by the legal people other than our names and ages as the Judge passed sentence on the innocent children before him.

Dad and Uncle Paddy had concocted a story which they were sure would get Danny excluded from incarceration in the Dreaded Artane Industrial school for boys over eight years old.

They used the fact that Danny was thirteen and nearing working age (fourteen then). Uncle Paddy said Danny was welcome to stay with him and his wife and children, just a few doors away from what was our family home. The story was accepted and Danny was spared. In reality he would return to our old home with Dad.

The Judge ordered that the girls be placed with the nuns. Leo too was to go to a convent, but not with us. In those days boys and girls were always kept separate. Betsy, our baby sister, was only twenty months old, Sheila was three-and-a-bit, and Leo was almost five-and-a-half.

On naming each child the Judge announced that they be placed in a place of safety until they reach their sixteenth birthday. The sentence for Bernie and myself seemed such a long time, we were eleven and twelve, but for the little ones it was an eternity. It was a blessing that the younger ones did not understand. I could not stop crying. It was a nightmare, the sheer savagery of splitting up a whole family. We four girls were taken to a room and locked in; we had no idea where Leo had been taken, though we found out later that it was to a place called Drogheda – that could have been in another country for all we knew. To this day the memory of how Leo was so cold-heartedly wrenched from us haunts us.

I had been like a little mother to him, he must have felt abandoned. I could not come to terms with the fact that it would be years before we would see him again – contact with siblings was not encouraged back in those days. As neither parent wanted any contact with the other, we were allowed to talk to them separately through a wire grid in the locked door.

My father spoke first, his only concern was that we understood that it was 'Mam's fault' that we were going away. Even a fool should know that it mattered little to us at that moment who was to blame.

We were still naive and innocent enough to hope that when Dad saw our distress that he would immediately go back to the Judge and promise that he would never beat Mam again and we could go home again and live happily ever after.

Mam cried uncontrollably and promised that she would never stop trying to get us back. I knew she meant it. I wanted so much to grab hold of her and be reassured that everything would be alright.

I lifted Betsy and Sheila up to see Mam, they were still bewildered and were obviously wondering why we were all in tears. That day of parting will never go away, I really believed that my heart would break.

Who were the faceless people who had decided that families were better separated than living with parents who were living in sin, they would know all about us. They had learned from Dad that Mam was living in sin and from Mam that Dad was about to as soon as his new lady was sure he had been granted a legal separation. We knew nothing of these things, all we were hoping for was to be with our mam, and have our brother with us.

The parting was obviously so stressful that the events leading up to our final place of incarceration are foggy. I remember that leaving the Court under escort and being guided into a dark-coloured car (as if in slow motion) I spotted a lady lifting Leo into another car and hoped that he was coming with us after all, that he was just travelling in a different car.

My next memory was that we were in a convent either in or on the outskirts of Dublin until a permanent place was found for us; I don't know if it was the place or the area, but 'Whitehall' rings a bell.

I have no memory of the journey to Athlone from Dublin, but recall entering the driveway though the black iron gates. My eyes were drawn to the grotto on the right and as we passed it I silently prayed to the Virgin Mary for help, I still believed in miracles!

The first days and weeks are a total blank, I believe this to be the result of trauma due to the family break-up.

Many of the girls were over twenty years old, who had stayed on due to having no one to go to. They would have been free to go by law, but were so institutionalised they had no direction. They were placed in charge of various groups. It took time to understand the accent of these girls, they spoke with verbal expressions which were unique to them. Many girls were small for their ages, no doubt from lack of nourishment.

Bernie and I were placed in the seniors group and Sheila and Betsy in the infants. Two of the three girls who were in charge of the infants would be better suited as prison wardens, the third was lovely – her name was Mary Biddy.

Apart from picking up the accent and using peculiar expressions we became part of this sad family of unfortunate girls, all placed here for various reasons. As time went on we would learn some things but we would never know the real stories behind the lives of these girls – many had been abandoned and knew absolutely nothing about their past, nor would they ever be bold enough to ask.

I would liken the pain in my heart to the pain of losing someone in death, that's exactly how it feels when you wrench siblings apart, the pain made worse for me personally being separated from my mother.

This Strange And Different Life

We were aware of resentment from some girls – these were girls who had no outside family contact, I suppose that is understandable.

The other noticeable thing was the lack of normal human contact such as putting an arm around each other or linking arms. Kisses and cuddles were never in abundance at home so I was not expecting any in this strange place, though I gave my little sisters hugs on occasions we were allowed to mix with them in the playground.

Nuns did have 'favourites'. It did not pay to be liked by a nun, and girls not favoured had their own way of dealing with 'pets' as there were mockingly called. There were few days when some girl was not pulling the hair from another. The kids with no known family were definitely treated worse than those with.

Sister Ursula and Sister Breeda were two main nuns in charge of our daily lives, but Sister Helen and Sister Thadeus who were teachers of domestic sciences helped out with overseeing baths and organising prayer assembly. I disliked them both equally. Most of the daily running of the kids' lives were by the older girls who had stayed on after their time. We thought that anyone staying on was not quite alright mentally. I had no understanding at that time of the word 'institutionalised'. I know now they deserved pity and not ridicule.

One of the biggest shocks to the system was the 'food'. We had never lived like lords but I had taken better slops to the pig lady in Inchicore than the swill we had to eat. I used to think back to when I collected the neighbours' leftovers, as well as our own, and sell it to the local pig farmer to earn the money for the Sunday afternoon matinee at 'The Core', our local cinema.

I never thought I would see the day when I could kill for that same food to eat myself. I was once overheard complaining about our slop food and was reminded by the nun in question that I was only a 'Dublin nobody'.

The Dreadful Food

Breakfast consisted of gruel, without salt or sugar, and on alternate days it was one chunk of bread and a mug of cocoa or tea, again without sugar.

Lunch was another chunk of bread and another mug of the same greasy drink. The drink was served by the passing along of several tin mugs which were usually very rusty, so the tea or cocoa had greasy rust floating on top. The grease was the result of the same watering cans being used to distribute the soup we had with dinner.

Lunch was not served in the dining hall. We would sit around in a circle on the veranda and take turns in walking up to the tray of bread chunks which would be at the feet of whatever nun was on duty. She would oversee that no one picked up more than their one piece of bread. We would become very impatient with having to wait our turn for the passing along of the mugs, very unhygienic, but the word had no meaning back then.

Dinner was the same every day, except that we had turnip more often than cabbage. This was served with a lump of fat or gristle and two or three little potatoes in their jacket – tough luck if the spud was rotten in the middle. The mug of 'soup' was just the water in which the so-called meat had been boiled without any seasoning whatsoever – it was simply hot, greasy, tasteless water.

I recall the many new kids who would not touch the food at first and would eventually finish up killing for it. There was no alternative, it was amazing that there was not regular food poisoning! But then, who knows what the many girls buried in the convent cemetery died from?

I have often wondered if the deaths of young girls who died in religious institutions were ever investigated. They were beyond reproach in the days when the Church ruled in Politics.

Cruelty

To be fair, I have to say that not all cruelty was inflicted by the nuns – most of it, especially on the babies, came from the carers. Then there were the senior girls who picked on the smaller girls, especially the weak.

The fear shown by little toddlers was hard to take, they spent so much of their time cooped up in their dingy little room with little daylight. Because of where their room was situated – in the centre of the building – there was no direct daylight, the only light came from a very low watt bulb.

The little ones were not encouraged to run around, so they

sat on low benches which were resting against the walls of the narrow room – it was easier for those in charge to keep the tots sitting.

During the better weather we were encouraged to take our young sisters outside with us, they always found it difficult to adjust to the daylight for the first few minutes. The little ones could at least feel safe for the time they were with me and Bernadette.

I used to pray really hard when we first entered Summerhill that someone would come and take us away and I remember wishing every time I saw a car pulling up to the front of the convent that it was coming for my family. I used to sit on the playground so I had a clear view of the entrance to the convent's front door.

It did not take me long to realise that in order to survive I was going to have to toughen up, I was far too timid. I was not alone in this respect. Most of the poor kids who had been there from birth walked like victims lowering their heads when they passed the known bullies. I did not quite fit that description, but then I had not been there from birth.

We seniors had hair inspection every evening on the veranda. This was done most times by Sister Breeda. The veranda was extended from the babies' dingy little room. Sister Breeda would stand there like a large oak tree with comb in hand and roughly go through the hair of each child. She always dug the comb into our heads roughly and woe betide any child who was found to have nits. There was never any verbal warning if you were unlucky enough to have them. She would just grab hold of your hair and punch you in the head or between the shoulder blades. I remember the soreness of trying to sleep on my back after such punches – the discomfort forced me to lie on my side.

Sister Ursula was not quite as bad on the occasions she took hair inspection, she would push us away with a lecture and encourage girls to inspect and clean each other's hair. We never had any kind of treatment for nitty heads.

Her lecture was usually to remind us of how lucky we were to have three meals a day and a comfortable bed to sleep on. It was obvious she had never slept on our beds! We were not given extra blankets in winter and were punished if we slept two in a bed for warmth. We were encouraged to offer our pain and suffering to God to atone for our sins. I wonder if they did likewise as they committed more sins than we ever did!

Over the years I have managed to find it in my heart to forgive the older girl tormentors. I can believe now that they themselves were probably once the 'tormented'. Forgiving the nuns comes harder, not only for their cruelty but for the things they pretended not to have seen.

Hygiene! What's That?

I felt great sympathy for Molly, the girl who cleaned the outside blocks of toilets. They were usually in a disgusting state, though this was not always because of the girls' dirty habits.

There was no regular supply of cleaning materials. The same old yard brush had to last for ages and Molly would have only one handbrush to do both blocks of toilets. The flushing system was diabolical and was out of order most of the time, but girls would still answer nature's call and use them whether they flushed or not, so you can imagine the state of the place.

It was not until near the end of my time in Summerhill that toothbrushes were introduced, though not toothpaste. We used soap or soot from the old boiler room, and we used the same water to clean our teeth as we had washed in.

If you think that was bad, then the sight of girls drinking from the toilets when they flushed would be more shocking. Oh yes, when you were thirsty, you drank from wherever you could. You have to remember that the two places where the water was clean was the bathroom and the kitchen – both were out of bounds and drinks were only served three times daily.

Our ignorance when it came to menstruation was frightening, we had never had any warning about it and no provisions were made. I was fortunate in that I was a late starter and only ever had to suffer on one occasion.

I had seen many soiled rags and paper but had no idea as to what or who had left the objects around the toilets. I once saw a girl leaving the classroom in great distress with blood-stained clothing, but thought that she had a bleeding injury and wondered why some girls sniggered at her.

I can recall the time it first happened, I kept it to myself and dealt with it on instinct alone. I suppose that the fact that sanitary wear was unheard of at this time can be seen as ignorance on the side of the nuns and by the same reckoning surely they themselves would have the same monthly problem.

The other amusing thing was (though not at the time) the embarrassment suffered by girls with larger breasts and the things we did in trying to hide them. Brassieres were not supplied, so some of us would select smaller chemises which helped to flatten our bosoms. Apparently in earlier days girls had been supplied with bodices, but there were not many available, not enough to go round for all who needed one.

The girls who had developed bosoms were those who would have come to the convent as older children and would have perhaps had some nourishment or at least a better diet, though I could never imagine one that could have been worse.

In order to add some humour to these memories I will give you an account of my first lesson on the birds and bees. I and a couple of my close friends were out of bounds on the farm when we heard voices and hid in the cow enclosure. The safest place was above in the hayloft and we lay there until it was safe to proceed on our way. The male voices grew nearer and suddenly two of the farmhands appeared below, ushering what we thought to be a cow into the enclosure below. There was already another cow tied to one of the fenced areas. We thought that these men were very peculiar as they forced the 'cow' to mount the other cow, and took quite some time in achieving this. There was no way we were going to be caught by such peculiar people so we stayed put for what seemed like an eternity. I still laugh to myself when I think back, unknowingly we had experienced the mating of two animals.

There were few girls who would dare get up to some of the things I did after I had been there a while, but they were conditioned to obedience, 'God Help Them'! I can only guess what their past lives had been like.

Looking back, I would say that my adventures, or distractions, were my way of keeping sane.

We worked hard, rising at six, and after dressing and going for a wee would say morning prayers before work in our dormitories. We would strip our beds and roll up the mattress and fold our bedding. We would then lift the iron beds to one side and get down on our knees and hand buff the highly polished floors, not missing an inch.

After Mass we would eat breakfast (that did not take long) and go to the veranda to wash. I was always baffled as to why we all had to wash in the same big tub of water at the far end of the veranda, when the bathroom had a row of handbasins down one side. We took turns walking to the big tin bath washing our hands and face in carbolic soap. When we were all washed the two biggest girls would lift the bath outside and dispose of it. We would then comb and inspect each other's hair until school time.

While I can see that to some people this may not appear to be such hard work, I would like you to consider that on a very poor diet and the fact that these girls were small for their ages, it was indeed hard work. Some girls who had long passed school age had some very hard and dirty jobs to do.

Did The Locals Know?

I will always have mixed feelings about the local people of Athlone Town. I can never quite accept that they were unaware of the suffering of children within the convent walls.

Some of the very local children were educated with us – they were known as externs. I had become friends with one girl whom I had persuaded to share her sandwiches with me; she eventually started to bring extra in her packed lunch and I did beg of her never to tell the nuns or I would be punished.

The externs never entered the institution so would be unaware of our conditions. This also applied to the teaching nuns who, even though they lived within the convent, saw very little of our lifestyle. There was one exception – her name was Sister

Benigna, she was very friendly with Sister Breeda and on rare occasions entered our domain to take charge of us for the Rosary.

Sister Benigna's classroom was next to ours, she taught a younger group. There was an incident one day during lessons when my teacher, Sister Incarnata, asked me to distribute some paperwork to our class. This task had very often been done by a girl called Angeline, so when I got to her desk she directed some name-calling to me. I had never liked the girl who, even though small for her age, had a nasty side to her and of course the fact that she came from Athlone town could have had some bearing on my dislike for her. As an immature girl I associated anyone connected to the town as distasteful as the institution, so I found it easy to smack her across the face and banged her head on the desk for good measure. My actions resulted in Sister Benigna in the adjoining classroom becoming involved and ordering me into her room.

She was not successful in extracting an apology from me to the sneering Angeline who had been brought in with us. When Sister Benigna's pushing me and hitting me on the arms did not succeed, she sent to the kitchen for her pal Sister Breeda. I tried hard to explain to Sister Breeda that I had only given the girl what she deserved and that my apology would not be sincere as I was not sorry.

My disobedience resulted in Sister Breeda grabbing my hair on both sides and banging my head on the wooden clad wall. Apart from my headache my head was also very sore, and on feeling something cold running down my neck I put my hand on the nape of my neck to discover blood. The red-faced nun realised she had banged my head on a single protruding nail, which obviously at some time had held a picture. She ordered me to her kitchen to have my wound seen to, and it was now my turn to sneer back at Angeline as she had done as she watched the nun trying to batter an apology from me to her.

Whatever Sister Breeda used to bathe my head caused smarting, but I was not going to flinch now at this stage – she simply gave me one of her usual shoves telling me to get out of her sight, I had got off lightly this time.

It was very apparent how disappointed Sister Incarnata was on my return to class as she beckoned me back to my place. I know for a fact that the punishment I received was not what she expected, she was the most gentle nun I have ever met.

From that time onwards I held Sister Benigna in great contempt, basically because she had involved one of the nastiest nuns to do her dirty work.

Sister Incarnata had done her utmost to direct my anger in other directions, such as studying, especially my favourite subject English. She was very aware how much I disliked Gaelic, I have always believed it should have been optional. In her attempt to help me, Sister Incarnata sought the help of a colleague of hers in another convent in Athlone town – her name was Sister Laurencia, she invited her to Summerhill and I later was allowed a return visit, she was as nice as my teacher. It was kind of Sister Incarnata to try and help me but I had never really acclimatised to life in the convent.

If there is such a place as 'Heaven' those two nuns will make it there. I have always felt that those two will have prayed for me every day of their lives. Sister Incarnata knew that basically, I was still that nice sensitive kid that had entered Summerhill surviving 'rightly or wrongly' the only way I could.

The Changing Me

Obviously I have no idea as to the time in my life or the first incident that started the change in my behaviour. It would not be possible to recall the order of any incident, though the pain of recalling them is as painful today as when they happened.

One of the nasty occasions that comes to mind took place on a Saturday morning (bath day) as I stood on the concrete floor outside the bath house with other girls, waiting our turn. We were chatting and holding on modestly to our chemises, when I heard my sister Bernadette scream out from within the baths. My instant reaction was to run inside and see what was happening. Sister Thadeus who was on bath duty that morning was beating Bernadette with the large thick stick she would normally patrol the cubicles with, usually tucked underneath her arm.

I had no choice other than get between the frenzied nun and my sister and help drag her from the bath, taking some of the lashes myself as I helped my sobbing sister outside to where she had left her clothes in a neat little pile. Apparently Bernadette had back-chatted the wretched nun during a needlework class earlier in the week, so she had taken the opportunity of punishing her when she was in a more vulnerable position – sitting in the bath.

It was times like this that filled me with such feelings of hatred, and made me question the teachings of the Church, especially the part that said nuns were 'Brides of Christ'.

I had known fear in my life before coming to this awful place, but had never felt so consumed by the feeling of hate. I suppose I came to the conclusion that the only thing to do was start making statements in my own way, such as becoming as disruptive as possible.

The brutality and deprivation within the convent walls was having a terrible effect on me and I could feel that I was even in conflict with myself, as though the person I really was, and the one I was trying to be, were at war. I would say the most serious act of defiance and disrespect towards a nun came one evening as Sister Helen was taking the evening prayers and Rosary and she sent another girl called Ann to fetch me from my duty of schoolroom cleaning.

I told the girl to tell Sister Helen that I would pray as I worked, but the girl returned again with the same order and my answer was the same. Sister Helen appeared at the door looking angry, ordering me to come to the veranda at once.

She lunged towards me as I carried on sweeping and before I knew what was happening I had the broomhead in the air, threatening her that I would knock her head off if she laid a hand on me. It was as though I was standing aside watching someone else do it and as she retreated out of the room towards the cloister in anger, I knew I would pay for my insane act.

In normal circumstances she was capable of dishing out her own punishment, but most times it would be Sister Breeda or Ursula who would punish.

It was as we queued for breakfast the following morning that I was called to step out and produce my open hand. I lost count of the number of whacks with her thick stick; I felt as though my hand was broken as I stepped back putting my hand under my left arm. I was also told to miss all three meals for the day.

Usually my time alone always in punishment turned to thoughts of Leo, wondering where he was and how he would cope with punishment. He had always been a wild free spirit who would go off wandering at the drop of a hat. He had kept me fit in Inchicore and Ballyfermot, it was always my job to go searching for him and carry him back with his legs over my shoulders. I used to wonder were the nuns where he was cruel to him or would he have moved on to Artane and was suffering the torment of the Christian Brothers – it did not bear thinking about, but it was hard trying not to think.

The Admiring Locals

I would be taking a wild guess in saying that there were about one hundred and fifty children in the convent and it stands within one mile of the town rather than two.

Every Sunday afternoon we were accompanied by either two nuns or two of the charge girls on a walk outside the grounds of the convent. We would turn either left or right and walk in circular direction taking us around the cemetery in Drum where most of the girls who had died in Summerhill Convent were buried. We would stop for a short time and offer prayers for their souls. It would be hard to imagine any of those unfortunates ever having committed sins.

The local people would look at us and give us piteous smiles and bow their heads in respect to the nuns.

We would play up more if it was charge girls escorting us than if it was nuns. One of the usual girls, Mary Dignam, was not too bad even if she did think she was gorgeous.

There were special walks we did on occasions such as Corpus Christi, Saint Patrick's day and Confirmation that took us into the town where we were admired by the locals like we were the circus coming to town, we could hear them praise the nuns for the good job they were doing. I suppose I should not pass scorn on the people, they may have been genuinely ignorant about institutions.

I have now become aware of how desperately short of money these places were, but I still think that the tiniest show of humanity and kindness would have cost nothing.

Family Visits

Mam and Jim visited when finances permitted; money was very short, and Jim was not finding it easy to get employment with accommodation. I never did ask Mum if she visited Leo for fear of causing her to feel guilty if she had not visited him.

They always took us away from the convent grounds out to open spaces and would have brought some food and drink for a picnic. I hated it when it was time to return to the convent.

Dad's visits were less frequent. I don't think he came more than twice in the three-and-a-half years of my time in Summerhill. I found his company uneasy, I was not full of questions for him as I was with Mum and he never took us from the convent – he always appeared to be in a hurry to get back to Dublin, perhaps seeing us in the ghastly place pricked his conscience.

Our brother Danno's visits were more frequent than Dad's. Dad would always send sweets with Danno, he got them from a friend who worked for Rowntrees in Dublin. I knew the man, he lived on the same road as we did in Ballyfermot.

I was full of questions of how my little gang of friends were and wondered if they remembered me or asked about us. I told Danno about our little sister who Mam and Jim had and how lovely and tiny she was and how envious I felt of her being with Mam. He did not have to say how unhappy he was, but it appeared that Dad, who did not often smack us, had started to hit Danno a lot and had also behaved badly towards Alice, the woman he was now living with. On one of Danny's visits I noticed his face was red and his eye puffy. Apparently Dad's friend had got the usual bag of chocolates for Dad to send down to us early in the week and Danno found them rather tempting each time he saw them in the cupboard and helped himself; Dad punished him for this.

We were usually in a low mood after Danno left, it lasted for a day or so, we then had to get back to the reality of where we were.

Yearly Visit By Government Inspector

The yearly visit from the Government Inspector was one big fix. The nuns knew when the inspector was coming and all the rusty tins and plates were hidden away out of sight.

I have vague memories of the inspector's name as being something like Mrs McQuaid or McDade. We had delft instead of tin, there was more meat for dinner and we had milk with the porridge (which was made thicker) and also the butter was spread on the bread rather than the usual little dot that you would sometimes (if you were lucky) find.

The other great excitement was having hot water to wash up the greasy delft with.

The other thing missing was the hitting sticks normally carried around under the arms of Sisters Ursula, Breeda, Helen and Thadeus. I don't know where they were kept during the visit.

Oh yes, those of us whose clothes were tatty would be given more presentable clothing, though none of us were ever really raggy. I am surprised that the inspector never asked to look in the locked cabinets in the dining halls.

The dining halls were cold unfriendly places. The long heavy tables stood on large reddish flagstones. We bigger girls sat in one hall while the juniors and big babies used the second. Sister Breeda stood between the two and roared at anyone who spoke.

It seems strange to most people who hear my story that so many people claim to have known nothing about such deprivation back then. It could be said that perhaps little could be done because of lack of funding, but not all homes were bad, or so I have been told.

The Secret Adventures That Made Life Bearable

There were a few children including mine who were lucky enough to receive parcels from relatives, ours came mainly from Mam's relatives. Gran Elizabeth and Mam's sister Lily sent us goodies including Gran's home-made cake. She was very good and had made wedding cakes for local people in her neighbourhood.

We were never allowed to have the complete contents at one time but spread the treat out over weeks. Bernie and I would take our little sisters' share and stay with them to be sure it was not taken from them – we usually went to a spot in the playground under a tree.

Bernie would also on occasions arrange for our very close friends to join us at our very private hiding place and share our goodies with them. To get to this place we had to make sure the coast was clear and meet on the top of the back stairway, this was three storeys up.

We would then have to climb onto a window ledge then on to the bannister rail, taking care not to fall to the flagstoned hallway below, to almost certain death. We then had to get on top of a cupboard and on to the large water cistern above.

The cistern was deep and half full of water, it had metal pipes just above the water level and wooden slats across on which we sat.

Above us was the bell housing. This bell was rung three times daily 6 a.m., 12 a.m. and 6 p.m. It seemed a long way down and the thick rope from the bell was out of arm's length, not that we would dare try to touch it.

We would giggle quietly and watch the kids and nuns pass below. Sister Ursula's office was less than halfway up the winding stairway and we kept very silent when she appeared either going to or coming from it.

There was an adjoining room to her office where all clothing was kept and repaired. It was a large storeroom, where I and other girls had helped out with the mending, especially the infants' clothes.

There was one occasion when we happened to be above in our secret place when the 'Angelus' rang out, the noise was deafening even with fingers in our ears.

If any of the nuns went into the office at a time when we needed to descend, we would remove our boots or shoes and quietly tiptoe along the top dormitory and down the stairs at the other end; we would then have to hope we met nobody who wanted to know what we were doing out of bounds. The risk added to the excitement. I admit that I often felt guilty at not sharing with all those unfortunate girls who never had parcels, but always eased my guilt by convincing myself that it was just not possible to share with everyone.

These treats for us grew less as time went on, but my little bunch of friends and I still went to our special hiding place.

I had been caught on one occasion walking along the cloister after coming from the back stairway, but told the nun that I had been to the chapel to pray. That was untrue at that time, but I did very often go and pray on my own. The chapel did have a warm feeling as the candle flames reflected on the glossy wooden floor.

Sometimes Mary, the girl in charge of our group, would make comments about my absence, but coming from the larger group there was less chance of being missed, though there were more children in the junior group than the seniors, the smallest group were the infants. I did thank God for the fact that I was never unfortunate to be in the convent from infancy – the mere sight of those babies would break your heart.

I used to pray to my favourite Saint and would ask why she allowed those babies to suffer. I hoped that these babies would not be affected in their lives and hope perhaps they may not remember the worst, though judging from the three younger members of my own family, this may not be the case.

Some Faces Remain Clear

Faces of close friends like Annie Lynch, Agnes Kelly, Patty Nugent, Vera Sheehan and Maura O'Shea have never faded nor have those of cruel people who were in charge including cruel nuns.

I clearly remember one little girl admitted to Summerhill shortly before I was released. She appeared to be about four years old. Her name was Winnie and she walked almost bent over and when she sat down she rocked back and forth continually.

Rumour had it that when she was born she was abandoned to an elderly relative who could not cope when she started to walk and apparently had to keep her strapped to a chair.

She spoke incoherently with a thick accent and so fast that it sounded foreign.

Her appearance drew lots of attention and my own curiosity got the better of me. I took the first opportunity to kneel down in front of her to see how long she could hold her head up and, as I placed my hand under her elfin chin, I gazed into the most beautiful eyes and her gorgeous little face was framed by lovely dark curly hair. I wondered how this unfortunate little bent beauty was going to survive in this damned place.

One of the most horrific things was witnessing how small children had learned to stifle their own cries of pain.

People who have asked why those of us who left did not report the cruelty – that's simple, nobody would have believed us, and there are still people even today in the twenty-first century who will not accept that these things happened in Holy Ireland. It will be years before many people will ever talk to anybody. I have tried and was always told "forget yesterday, look to the future." Maybe if I was not left with the legacy of a brother left physically and mentally crippled, a sister mentally disturbed and another younger sister who has battled with her feelings after fourteen years in the same institution as myself and Bernadette. My once wild little brother is now a timid recluse who prefers his own company. He says little, but the picture tells its own story.

61

Another girl called Mary came to Summerhill some time after we did. She was positive her mother would be back for her within weeks. She had an American accent and it appeared her 'mom', as Mary called her, had parted from her dad. When things were sorted she would be back for Mary.

Mary was a very chatty kid, about eleven or twelve with blonde almost curly hair and blue eyes. She had protruding teeth with thick pink lips that looked as though she wore lipstick. Her flashing eyes gave the impression she was always smiling. She soon became friendly with my sister Bernie.

Mary's haughty attitude amused Bernie – she thought Mary was like a breath of spring, but her attitude was not appreciated by other girls. She was not backward in her criticism of the speech, clothing we wore and most of all 'the food' – the kids in Summerhill suffered from lack of it, but poor Mary was going to learn the hard way! My sister and I were at her age when we entered, so we took it upon ourselves to try and help her adapt.

Mary had no doubt been loved and cared for and I have no doubt that her mother really believed she would be in the safest place. She may have been brought up in a typical Irish Catholic home, brainwashed and blinkered before going off to live in America.

When I left Summerhill Mary had settled, she still had a lot to say, but deep down she was very sensitive and could be reduced to tears easily.

People who would have voluntarily left their children within the convent can be forgiven if they judged the place by the entrance hall. Summerhill Convent entrance had a unique smell, the highly polished floors and the feeling of tranquility would give reassurance. We will never know if the parents who had to leave their children would have been in a position to do any other.

Sheila's Punishment For Bed Wetting

I can only guess that it was about eighteen months into our incarceration that I experienced pain and anger beyond explanation. As myself and the other girls who shared Sister Brigid's Dormitory (which was the only one left open day and night) lay awake chatting quietly, we were startled by a shriek from the infants' dormitory on the floor below.

We were used to distressed cries, but within seconds I recognised the scream that followed as that of the older of my two baby sisters – Sheila. I must have taken flight down to the door of the dormitory and peered straight through the large keyhole of the locked door to see Bernadette O, one of the carers, beating my young sister and chucking her like a rag doll, hitting her head off the circular metal headrail.

The dormitory was divided in two parts – Sheila's bed was the first bed in the middle row of the dormitory furthest away.

I could only cry and scream frantically and ran down to the cloister screaming, knowing the nuns were in the chapel, just feet away.

As expected, my disturbance brought Sister Ursula from prayer and I was ordered to be silent. I managed to make myself understood and she went to unlock the infants' door. I was ordered to return to my dormitory but I wanted to see my sister and hopefully lunge at the evil woman who had inflicted the terrible beating on my sister. I did not get the chance to do either. Instead I was threatened with punishment if I did not return to my bed.

On reflection, it was insane of me to think I could match up to the perpetrator – she was big and strong almost like a man, she could have put me on the floor with one punch.

It was hard to watch this creature stand there innocently after what she had done, and worse still that the nun spoke normally to her and obviously accepted whatever story she had given. The nun did not mention the incident again.

I had to try and sleep that night knowing that my little sister, who needed comforting, was locked in with a vicious woman who had half killed her for wetting her bed.

Sheila had always been a very docile child, she had always been a very good baby, but she became very withdrawn and kept her head bowed.

Even though there were three infant carers, only two slept in the same dormitory at night. Unfortunately Bernadette O was one of them; she also did work on the farm in the morning, it was just a pity she did not stay there permanently.

I had never seen violence inflicted on children so young until I came to this cursed place. During my visits to the chapel I used to ask St. Theresa to tell St. Peter not to allow some of the nuns and carers in when their time on earth was over.

It has always baffled me as to why the small children's dormitories were locked anyway, I had never heard of anyone stealing children.

It had taken years to rid myself of the guilt for not exacting revenge on the woman who inflicted such cruelty on Sheila and I am trying still to remember that one of my sister's tormentors was once the tormented. The nuns had a choice of where they wanted to spend their lives!

Confirmation Day

After much preparation and religious instruction, Confirmation Day came.

I was older than the average girl to be confirmed, but was looking forward to the occasion, not because of the religious aspect, simply because of the expected treat afterwards.

The local people came out to view us as we made the procession to the church in Athlone Town. They nodded and smiled at us and commented to each other about how lovely we all looked. I had chosen the name Therese as my Confirmation name, after my favourite Saint.

I remember feeling like a human being again as we walked towards the town's convent. It was a finishing school for older girls and it was a long standing custom to invite the girls from Summerhill back to their dining hall for a special tea on Confirmation Day.

It was easy to become dehumanised during incarceration and the feeling I felt as people spoke and handed us goodies felt great.

The older girls from the host convent had impeccable manners. To be honest I felt quiet inadequate, though this would have been the last thing that these girls would have wanted. One of the nuns from this convent, Sister Laurencia, was a close friend of my favourite teacher in Summerhill – Sister M. Incarnata. I became very down when it was time to leave and return, this place was so different and had such a happy atmosphere. It would have been nice to have had some photographs of the wonderful occasion, truly a day to treasure.

Working In The Kitchen

By the age of fourteen or so, I had all but given up on my education and was doing more kitchen work than anything else.

It may have been decided that because of the change in my behaviour it was best to keep me occupied and I believe in those days that education was only compulsory up to the age of fourteen.

On reflection, I believe that my anger blinded me to the importance of Academic achievement.

Working in the kitchen did have some advantages, such as discarding some rotten potatoes that would otherwise have been dished up to us for dinner. After all there was no such thing of complaining or asking for replacements for rotten potatoes, to do so would result in a thump around the head and to be asked "Who do you think you are?"

There were occasions when I had the chance of grabbing the odd scraps of food for my sisters and the little girl I had taken under my wing to save her from one particular bully who picked on her a lot. I had disliked this one particular bully from the time she smacked my sister Sheila across the face for fighting with another of the infants in her own group. I recall waiting some time for the chance to pay the bully back. I took the opportunity one evening as the girl called Margaret was sitting in the veranda having her hair combed and inspected prior to our inspection by Sister Breeda.

I grabbed hold of the hair that had been combed over her eyes, dragged her to the floor and hit her many times, drawing blood. The girl named Philomena whom I had rescued from this bully repaid me by mending my socks and cleaning my shoes; she did not have to, it was her way of thanks. The funny thing was that Philomena was not much younger than I, but she was very tiny as were most of the kids who had been malnourished from infancy. I had never known Philomena to have letters or visitors.

I have often wondered who felt the most depravation and have come to the conclusion that it must have been kids like my family, meaning the older members, after all we had things to compare life with.

The head girl in the kitchen, named Joan, was quite easy-going, but did not worry when she transferred the potatoes from the rinsing water into the big cooking pot – she could plainly see that many were rotten, but she was conditioned to convent life.

There was little anyone could do when the so-called meat was put on to cook. I believe it was about sixty per cent fat and gristle. Even though Joan was very much in charge of things in the kitchen, food was never served unless Sister Breeda was present – perhaps it was part of the perverted pleasure she got from feeding us slop that compelled her to be present!

Mattress Making

Apparently this was a chore which only took place every couple of years, and thank Heaven I only had to suffer the horrible chore once during my stay in Summerhill.

I will never forget the awful discomfort of trying to breathe, and trying not to scratch proved impossible.

Sister Thadeus and Sister Helen alternated on the oversee-ing of the dirty job. Several mattresses would be taken to the laundry and the ends of the stitching hand-picked by a couple of girls and the horsehair stuffing removed and given to two other girls who would tease the stuffing apart and feed into an old iron antiquated machine. The dust filled the laundry and we all coughed and sneezed and scratched non-stop, drawing blood at times.

Luckily there was water within reach, though we still only drank when the nun in charge was out of the laundry for a break. Two other girls would help the nun in charge wash the covers and put them in the big old drier after they were mangled. It was important to get the complete job done within the day as they had to be back on the beds by night – there were no spares.

The fiddly part of the job was putting back the rag round buttons with twine and a very large needle – there were six on the small mattresses and ten on the bigger ones; we would knot the threaded twine and put it through, pulling it tightly through and put another round button on the opposite side, pull tightly and knot the other side.

Ideally we should have been allowed to bath after such a dirty job, but we were only allowed to rinse our face and hands. We would suffer with thirst and risk getting caught out of bounds at night for a drink. Apart from pooh-shovelling in the outside toilets this is the worst job I have ever done. Discomfort in the extreme!

The Missing Office Key

Although Sister Ursula walked with an air of majesty, she looked every bit the jailer with the large bunch of keys hanging from the wide black belt around her waist. Most of the doors were very sturdily made with large keyholes and keys.

I did an awfully stupid thing, but at the time it was done on impulse after Sister Ursula entrusted me with the keys to the office. I cannot remember now what it was she asked me to fetch for her, but clearly recall her holding the bunch of keys, having singled out the key to the office – it was a Yale type. I had wanted a stamp as I had written a pitiful letter to Mam and did not want it to go through the normal procedure of censorship; I knew that stamps were kept somewhere in one of the drawers in the desk but felt too nervous to rummage and left the office and locked it.

I took off the key and gave it to Bernie telling her to go to the office during a period when she knew that all nuns would be at prayer. I told Bernie to hide the key under the mat at the bottom of the stairs leading to the office after she had taken the stamp. She reluctantly agreed. I could see she was nervous. I was stupid enough to think it would be assumed the key had fallen off the bunch and landed under the mat. I knew it would be found by one of the two girls whose job it was to clean those stairs early in the morning before Mass.

I was puzzled that nothing happened before Mass, as I knew that these girls would have wasted no time in handing their find to Sister Ursula. Sister Ursula was standing outside the chapel door as we came out and ordered the senior girls to stand to one side while she directed the others to the dining hall. She lost no time in requesting that the thief came forward or everyone would be punished.

I was very confused, did she not recall who it was that she had entrusted with the keys? Or was she testing my honesty? My mind was working overtime wondering what to do, when Sister Ursula threatened that everyone would go without food and, fearing that Bernie would confess, I stepped forward.

Sister Ursula did not look for reasons to use the cane, but when she did use it, there was no holding back! After six lashes on my right hand, I refused to take any more, and was immediately ordered down to the dark room below. I received another lash on my shoulder as I turned to walk away. Everyone in sight was ordered not to give me anything to eat for the rest of the day.

As I stepped into the dark room the thick red door was bolted behind me and I sat down on the cold concrete floor until my eyes adjusted to the darkness. I tried to relieve the pain from my right hand by placing it on the cold floor. I thought my right shoulder was broken.

The room that confined me was part of an area known as the 'cooking school' – why, I don't know, perhaps there had been a connection in past times. Behind another red door within the room was our bathhouse. Unfortunately it was locked, so a drink was out of the question. Eventually the room appeared lighter as the sun came through the gaps around the doors.

Luckily the bathhouse had a glass roof which helped, most of the daylight came from that door. There was a very small window that looked out on to the enclosed veranda, this window was covered in wire mesh. I could hear the chatter from the little children in their dingy room adjoining the veranda. My hand and shoulder still hurt but it was nothing compared to the lives of those little souls.

I was very hungry by the afternoon but did not get any opportunity of scrounging, even though I was permitted out to go to the toilet. I knew that someone would keep me some morsel from their own meagre ration of food. I had cause to laugh at myself for being afraid that I might have a visit from a rat – even they were not stupid enough to come where there was never any hope of finding as much as a crumb.

It may seem silly that I went through such severe punishment for a mere stamp, after all, the letter to Mam telling her about our unhappy plight would only make her miserable. There was nothing she could do, but we needed to tell someone.

I was released in time for the evening Rosary, and found that Bernie and her friend had kept me a couple of cold potatoes and a very hard piece of bread.

I have been asked why I never wrote to the authorities in Dublin. Firstly I would not have known who to write to and secondly, I would not have trusted the establishment to care. There is no doubt in my mind that the people in power were aware of the plight of kids in Ireland's homes, they simply did not give a damn.

On Better Terms With Sister Breeda

By this time I was on better terms with Sister Breeda and at times considered her to be almost human, though I still approached her with caution. The expression on her face did not always let you know what sort of frame of mind she was in.

It was on an occasion when it was her turn to do the 'wake up duty' at 6 a.m. one morning that I saw the compassionate side of her. I was unable to get up because of the fact that my thighs were stuck together due to a weeping rash.

My legs had become irritated by the material my skirt was made from. Unfortunately my chemise was not long enough to protect me, so because of my scratching it got worse by the day. Not having joined the others for prayer in the larger dormitory next door, Sister Breeda came looking for me.

I had pulled myself up to a sitting position and pulled my legs to the floor – it caused pain to try and part my legs. I was shocked by her sympathetic gaze as she asked me if I could hop the few yards to the sick bay which was an extension to our dormitory. She told me she would return after prayers to help me and to make myself comfortable on one of the beds.

I remember having some sort of solution poured between my thighs and was advised to look away as she forced my legs apart quickly. I felt sick and tried not to show that I was bawling. I felt quite silly as the tears ran down my face, made worse by Sister Breeda's show of sympathy.

I felt very embarrassed as she lifted my bowed head and said, "Come on now, Murphy, it's okay for a 'toughie' to cry."

I needed a dressing for a few days but then had to allow the air to get to my legs. I was excused work duties and had to wear longer-legged knickers for some time afterwards. The hope that I would not have to endure further stays in the Infirmary were short lived.

My sister Sheila had developed a large lump on the top of one side of her head and Sister Ursula ordered me to stay with her in the Infirmary attached to St. Bridget's dormitory; she was to be treated by Sister Breeda who attended to all medical needs. I have no memory of a doctor ever attending any child for ailments.

I was given no explanation as to what caused Sheila's lump and never looked while she did whatever she did to treat the lump. I know that Sheila made very little fuss, but she had always been a good baby and had been an easy baby to rear.

The sick bay was a very quiet place during the day and, with little to do other than talk to my little sister, time dragged. It would have helped to have something to read or games to play but the convent had never had children's toys or books. Sheila did not complain as she had my full attention and she had always felt safe with me.

I suppose I will never know what had caused the large fluid-filled lump to come up on my sister's head and at the time gave little thought to the possibility of the beating for bed-wetting punishment having caused it. I do remember that after the swelling shrunk, Sheila's normally straight hair became curly on one side.

St. Bridget's Dormitory, on the third storey and last floor up, was also used on occasions for visits from the dentist. I remember them well. I remember the sound of our extracted teeth as they were discarded into the metal bucket. I wonder if the reasoning for using the particular dormitory for this purpose was to avoid others from hearing the screams.

Preparing Bernie To Take Over As Magpie

I had become familiar with lots of nooks and crannies around the convent and its grounds, not so much in the nun's area, there were only a very select few who were allowed to work in the nun's quarters – girls who the nuns would have earmarked as prospective candidates likely to become nuns.

By now I had been encouraging Bernie to join me on more of my adventures. I needed to prepare her to take my place as magpie to provide extras for the family after my departure from Summerhill.

This is not as calculating as it sounds, it was instinctive and I had needed these distractions to keep my sanity. I can put my hand on my heart and swear that I was not a born thief. Today I am one of the most trustworthy people you are likely to meet. I am very serious about that.

Apple scrumping was a distraction that I enjoyed, made more exciting by the fact that the orchard was out of bounds to the children. We did it late at night when the convent was in total darkness.

To do this was easy from St. Bridget's, but had been much more fun when I had been in the larger dormitory of St. Anne's.

Our charge girl's bed was placed quite near to the fire escape exit, which meant we had to be as quiet as mice.

The orchard was alongside the maze of hedged walkways where the nuns walked and prayed during the day. It was an eerie place to be in the dark, as the orchard was right next to the nun's burial ground.

We walked very close together, giggling and tittering as we spoke in whispers, not because anyone was likely to hear us but out of respect for the dead. We came prepared with pillowcases from our beds. We found our adventure very exciting and found we could forget any bad happenings of the day. We could laugh and enjoy scaring the wits out of each other. It is amazing how darkness can play tricks on your imagination. I do believe that every scary ghost story I had ever been told would come to mind in these situations.

I remember crawling around on hands and knees in the orchard for fallen apples when I touched what was obviously a hand. Not only did I and the girl whose hand I touched let out a deathly scream, so did the others. I explained that I thought it was the hand of one of the dead nuns.

In the cold light of day it was clear that there was some distance between the orchard and the nun's burial ground, but the darkness coupled with our guilt of being out of bounds all added to our innate belief in superstition.

It was hard trying to muffle our laughter and tittering on the way back to the playground to reach the fire escape. We had to go very quietly and not disturb any of the other girls especially Mary, our charge girl.

We did not at this time sleep adjacent to each other, but were close enough to whisper back and forth. We found it very hard dropping off to sleep with all the excitement and we all had the same problem of trying not to laugh out loud at the memory of events in the orchard, stifling the laughter was physically painful. I have never really seen our act as stealing the apples, after all they were fallers and would have just rotted and been eaten by birds and worms. I am convinced we were more deserving.

The Retreat

Although hunger and thirst was something we lived with daily, it was the thirst that bothered us most, especially during the summer months.

There was a particular time every summer when the nuns wanted silence for their Prayer Retreat. The juniors and seniors would be herded up the local hills adjoining the convent. The nuns would honour a vow of silence and would speak only when absolutely necessary and then it was only in a whisper, usually directed to the older girls in charge, and was usually in connection with the daily running of the place. This was one period when the older girls would be almost in full control of our welfare.

I was lucky enough to have only suffered two summers on the hill due to Mam taking us for holidays to where she worked in Dublin.

There was little shade on the hill as there was more shrubbery than trees and permission to go to the local shop had to be given by our charge girl.

Not many girls had money to spend but I was a good saver and would hang on to any monies given to me by family visiting or sent by Auntie Lily or Gran.

Permission to go to the shop would normally be given by Sister Ursula, but during retreat it was Mary our charge girl. I must admit that I did not always ask for permission and on these occasions would go to the playground on the pretence of going to the lavatory.

I would get under a mesh fence and crawl along the pathway that ran alongside and to the gateway that led to a lane, and could only stand up when I could be hidden by the shrubbery and hedge of the lane. From there it was only yards from Lennon's shop. The windows that faced the playground were only dormitory windows on the upper floors and those of the closed veranda below. They were the most likely that someone would spot you from, so great care and observation was taken during illegal trips to the shop.

The problem with asking permission from the charge girl during the Retreat was that she would expect some of my goodies, and I could find more deserving cases than her to share with. Access to the lane was much easier from the hill, than from the convent itself.

I must admit that I took more risks than most of the girls were prepared to take. I often ventured down to the farmyard and fetched back dirty water from the pigs' trough – thirst drove me to desperate measures. Girls were known to pee in their shoes and drink their own urine. I had tried it once but could not develop a taste for it. I had a strong will and found myself using all the cunning within to survive.

I have to say that the visit to the little shop was more enjoyable when I had gained permission, simply because of the ease at which I could stroll and use my imagination. I would pretend that I was still in the cottage in Blessington with Mum and the little ones and imagine that Mam had sent me to the local shops. I could also sit and delay my return and often waved to the local people out working in the field. There were girls who thought that I was brave because of the risks I took by going out of bounds. I was not brave, I had spent more time in the world outside than they had and I had not been as conditioned as they were.

I do not mean that as a put-down to these girls – I suppose I could say that I was simply luckier, that's all!

There was one occasion when our charge girl, Mary, was sitting too near my escape route and I was compelled to ask her permission to visit the shop. I did not have much to spend and told her so, in the hope that she would not expect any of my sweets.

I was unable to afford anything to drink, so decided that I would return the long way back via the farmyard in the hope of finding a container to fill with water from the animal trough.

It was good to walk without ducking and diving in case of being spotted, though I did have to take care as I sifted through the tip for any discarded turnips as I had to compete with very large rats. They could always be found nearby and of course even though I had permission for my absence I was off track and if spotted in the farm area would be in line for punishment after the Nun's Retreat.

I found a filthy bottle and washed it in the trough before filling it very carefully, trying not to get any small maggots in.

I was quite pleased to return and find Mary engrossed in conversation with a girl from Dublin who had been sent to Summerhill for not attending school. Her name was Maura, she was lovely.

Maura had very caring parents who sent her lots of parcels and letters. Mary was in awe of Maura who appeared much older than she was. Maura had a beautiful singing voice which gained her much admiration from the nuns.

Maura was very fond of my family, biased maybe, because we were Dublin kids too. She would always defend Bernie and I if we were in conflict with the others, and in our charge girl's eyes Maura could do nothing wrong, though Maura had a temper that would bring a hush to the noisiest quarrel.

I was very cunning and approached our carer while Maura was present, showing her what little I had got for my money and of course she dismissed me and did not expect anything. It was after Maura's admission that Mary paid less attention to where I or my friends were.

Though Maura was tough she never went looking for confrontation with anyone, in fact she had a very soft side to her and cried in my company many times. She had a little brother whom she missed dreadfully, his name was Emmanuel.

I think it only fair to say that not all the very senior girls were cruel and nasty. Our charge girl was not too bad, a little fickle maybe, but I always did my best to avoid her when she displayed outbursts of temper.

I do believe that having regular contact with relatives made a difference to how kids were treated overall, and those who had no contact with family had the worst time. They were 'the forgotten' children.

Nancy D. who had charge of the juniors was quite a nice human being – not perfect by any means, but was able to keep control without violence.

There were three who shared the care of the infants – Patricia K., Bernadette O. and Mary B. If I could have chosen who cared for the little ones, my choice would have been Mary B. and Nancy D.

I would have liked to see Patricia K. and Bernadette O. work as rat catchers on the farm and sleep there also. They were not fit to have any control over the helpless infants.

The Lovely Mary B.

I can honestly say that the face of Mary B. is the one that has stayed clearest in my memory. I was not in regular contact with her but spent many occasions chatting with her.

I suppose she and her younger sister Betty had been in Summerhill since childhood. I had never seen them have visitors, nor did they go out on holiday (not to my knowledge anyway).

There were rumours that they were in some way related to Sister Breeda, though she showed no outward favouritism toward them. I remember an occasion when I helped Mary B. sort out some children's clothing in the supply room.

One of the things she told me was that some day she would marry a farmer and have six children, she was so innocently funny. I would imagine that she knew as much as I did about how babies were made – absolutely nothing!

At this time there was no reason that I knew of why Mary B. could not fulfil her dreams, though I have to admit that marriage and having babies was the last thing I ever wanted. Freedom and food were my priorities at that time.

My next memory will remain with me forever.

I was walking along the cloisters and spotted Mary B. carrying the trays with the babies' food and was about to go out to take one of the trays from her when she was called to the small kitchen window that looked out on the courtyard. Sister Breeda appeared to be talking normally one minute and then suddenly reddened and made a swipe at Mary B. By this time I was standing out of sight and though I was watching I could not hear what was being said.

I stood in the cloister opposite, knowing it was not a sensible place to be caught as there were several places from where a nun could appear and ask me what I was doing. I cannot explain why I was unable to drag myself away from the sight of Sister Breeda grabbing hold of Mary B's hair and banging her head from side to side on the window.

After what seemed like an eternity, the red-faced nun let go and Mary came rushing in my direction and I ran up the first flight of the spiral stairway that led to the dormitories and Sister Ursula's office. She was not in her office at this time, nor in the long workshop adjacent to it.

I stood and watched the bedraggled Mary B. rest the two trays on the bottom of the stairs and take hold of the bottom of her pinny and spit on it to wipe away her tears. She then gently put her fingers through her tousled hair, wincing as she did so and turned and went in towards the babies' dingy room.

I could not let the poor girl know that I witnessed the beating she had received from the frenzied nun – she would have been embarrassed. I never did discover the reason for the savage beating, nor if she ever told her sister Betty. I do not recall ever having another conversation with Mary B, nor do I know how much time elapsed between the beating and my class being asked to pray for her because she was very sick.

She was not in the small sick bay in my dormitory but in the old bigger one above the dining rooms. As this was Sister Breeda's domain it was unlikely that many would have had the chance of visiting Mary B.

From where I sat in the dining room I witnessed Sister Breeda having to rush up the stairs accompanied by Joan the head kitchen girl, who helped her lift Mary B. because she fell out of her sick bed.

I paid one unauthorised visit to her sick bed, but she did not recognise me and spoke incoherently. I recall the feeling of doom as I walked away from her bed towards the door that led to the back stairs that went down to the junior dining hall. Thinking that I heard someone coming, I dived into what turned out to be a very dismal bathroom that did not appear to have been in use for many years. It had no light bulb, or window and smelt musty.

There was another doorway just past Mary B's bed but that led to the nun's quarters, so the only exit for me was down the stairs and through the dining hall and, feeling very scared by now, I decided to just run and face the music if I was caught. Luckily Joan in the kitchen was chatting to another girl and I headed back to the veranda.

The older children attended Mary B's funeral. She was buried in Drum Cemetery which is very close to the convent, it was a very sad occasion.

Many rumours followed her death. Some said that she turned black all down one side of her body, but we were never informed as to why she died so young. I know it is possible that she may have had some terminal illness that we were not aware of or an inherent disease that ran in the family. I don't suppose we will ever know, but I will always be haunted by the fact that she died after the beating.

I have vowed that when I can feel comfortable with visiting that horrible place, Summerhill, I will find her resting place and pray for her and all the unfortunates who lived and died in that Institution.

No Apparent Odd Behaviour

A lot of stories have come to light about unnatural acts and hanky-panky between nuns and priests but, to be honest and fair, I do not think I have witnessed it. But that is not to say it did not go on.

There was an occasion where I was sent to a nun's cell (as they called their rooms) to stain the floorboards and I was

shocked to find how barren it was. The room was medium sized
with an iron bed in the centre of the room and on the wall
above the bed hung a black crucifix. There was a small ward-
robe and a little table with a bowl and jug, and there was nothing else hanging on the walls. I had been told that nuns were not
allowed mirrors, because of the sin of vanity.

The nuns did take care of their own rooms, it was rare that
we were asked to do their jobs for them. There were two girls
called Gertie and Anne who did spend a lot of time working in
the nun's dining area and kitchen. I never saw that part of the
convent. To this day I will never accept that becoming a priest is
a special calling. Pressure is more like the reason. Irish people
back then really saw it as an honour to have either a priest or
nun in the family and to have both gave them an air of superior-
ity. The stories of priests and nuns and hanky-panky is also something I have never seen. The nearest we saw them together was
on the altar when they played the part of the altar boys, during
Mass. I believe the presbytery was outside the grounds and a
couple of our girls would help with the priests' housework.

I suppose our innocence would have meant that having no
incline of sexual behaviour we would not have recognised it if
it did happen. Again, I have to say that these are my memories;
it was a big place and my account is about my depravation.

St. Brigid's Dormitory

This was a dorm that 'fourteens' and over slept in, the other
seniors slept in St. Anne's. I liked St. Brigid's as it was never
locked. The dorm was L-shaped and had twenty-two beds –
eighteen of those were in three rows; each row had six beds and
the smaller side had two beds either side of the door that went
into the six beds partitioned off as the sick bay.

There was another door in the small end that led to the nun's
quarters and on the right of the door was a large medicine cabi-
net. It was always locked and the keys held by Sister Breeda.
The black iron beds stood very uniformly with each mattress
rolled up and blankets folded neatly with a pillow on top. The

highly polished floors reflected everything around.

I slept on the second bed on the first row and there was a long row of marble stone topped wash basins the whole length of the dorm, but they were not connected to the water supply nor did they have taps. Perhaps it was a job started in the past and was never completed.

I was scared rigid of the rats that would run along the gullies underneath which was about two feet from my bed. On one occasion I was woken by the weight of a rat walking all over my body. We very often lay awake for hours with the noise of a rat gnawing away at the floorboards.

I was awoken one night by movement under my mattress and jumped into my friend Annie's bed. It was taboo to be caught in anyone's bed and Annie warned me to be out before hand clap at 6 a.m. She was very cranky in the morning from me disturbing her and asked me if I had food under my mattress. I assured her I had nothing. I was glad that Annie was gone to the lavatory when I discovered that I had wrapped some potatoes in a rag for my sister Bernie in St. Anne's dorm. I had not given them to her before her dorm was locked. I never did confess to Annie – she would have been grumpy with me for ages.

There are many funny memories of events shared with other girls, even though I still wince at those of sharing my bed with rats.

I suffered frequently with a sore throat and would feel more thirsty at these times. I was on my way to my dormitory one evening when I spotted Sister Helen's water bottle on the window sill. The entrance to the nun's cells was next to the entrance to St. Brigid's and I knew that the nun would pick up the bottle much later after evening prayers and fill it with hot water on her way back.

I sat on the steps and undid the water bottle and started to gulp down the water. The other girls who were eagerly awaiting turns to swig from the bottle fell about at the sight of me retching as I spat the foul tasting water into the wash-basin nearest to me.

Even after putting the top back and replacing the bottle back on the window ledge, I was still trying to control my retching. I can only liken the experience to the time I had tried sampling my own urine.

Initially I was angry that the girls found my discomfort so amusing, but when the horrible taste wore off I could see the funny side of it.

I was going to say that the wash-basin had never before had liquid disposed of through it until I remembered that there were many occasions when St. Anne's (which housed the nearest toilet) was locked, the girls of St. Brigid's used them to pee. Now that I come to think of it, I had always thought that the Jeyes fluid in hot water that was occasionally deposited in the gully was to try and dissuade the rats from running up and down, but perhaps not!

The Porridge Incident

I went to work one morning on the farm, not that it was part of my early morning workload but my charge girl Mary had agreed to me leaving my dormitory duties and helping Bernadette Oakley on the farm. I was quite happy to have the change from buffing the door floors. The older charge girl gave me my orders of what to do as she went off to another part of the farm. She would be back in time for morning Mass.

I went about the chore of sweeping the yard, and filling various buckets up with water from the big trough of water outside the laundry window.

I had been ordered to keep an eye on the large cauldron of gruel which was left hanging above the turf fire on a hook which was placed over an iron bar that went from one side of the hearth to the other.

The charge girl who worked on the farm was also part-time carer with two others to the infants. It was not easy working with the same girl who had beaten my little sister so badly, but at least she was elsewhere on the farm.

I went to the little farm kitchen type room to stir the gruel and stirred it as I had been told to do. As chicken food, it looked no worse than what we had to eat so, as it was bubbling, I decided to try lifting it off the hook.

I grappled with the heavy cauldron by wrapping old rags on either side and lifting it upwards to unhook it. As I found my hand burning I released the cauldron very quickly to the floor causing it to splash on to my face and legs.

I rolled down my black knee-length wool socks, trying not to scream with the unbearable pain, and ran towards the water trough. I threw the water all over my face and legs but it only eased the terrible burning. I felt very sorry for myself and had not even tried to taste the porridge as intended when it had cooled. It was my plan to allow it to cool and then eat as much as I could.

There was little sympathy from the carer when she returned, she warned me to keep it to myself and not look for treatment as she would be told off for letting me lift it.

I wondered if my face looked as red as it felt, and kept my head bent during Mass. I cupped my hands and kept blowing to try and cool my face; my legs were smarting too but with socks soaked with water, it helped. We both headed back to church for Mass. I really felt that the statue of St. Therese was accusing me as I raised my head to pray to her.

This was one occasion that I could not wait to do the washing up after breakfast, I needed to get more water for my face and legs which luckily did not blister.

I knew only too well that I must not seek treatment, after all my little sisters were in the care of the girl who had warned me to keep quiet.

On reflection, I regret opting out of education and firmly believe that the teaching of Gaelic in schools held many children back. Far too much time was dedicated to trying to force a language we were not born to, it should have been optional.

I admire the change in attitudes of many of the younger Irish generation and how less blinkered they are. They are more outspoken and can take criticism as well as give it, and are nowhere near the past generations on the hypocrisy scale. I liken some of the older generation to the Germans who refused to believe in the holocaust.

Wherever I have brought up the question of the nuns' and Christian brothers' cruelty with the older Irish folk and that includes members of my mother's family, they want to shush me up.

I grew tired of them telling me that my siblings' tormentors did their best. While I do not want to generalise I still say that, like the powers of the day, their heads were buried deeply in the sand.

Three Attempts At Escape

During my stay in Summerhill I had made three attempts at running away. The first was a very short-lived event as I had been spotted by the farmhand – he marched me back.

I was summoned before Mother Superior who reminded me that she had not requested my stay at the school; she told me how grateful I should be. How could I ever agree with that?

My second attempt took me further, I almost made it into Athlone Town but had stopped to rest on the wall of a big house. I had no idea what direction I should take when I reached the town.

I had been spotted by the lady of the house – her name was Mrs Cunningham. She mentioned that I had been sitting a long time and invited me in for tea. I did not hesitate in answering her questions. I readily told her that I was running away from a terrible place. She appeared very sympathetic and left the room while I tucked in to tea and cake. I started to imagine myself living here as a maid, I know lots of girls went out to service. I did not realise that the voice I had heard was not the lady speaking to someone in the house – she had been on the phone. It was not long before Biddy Graham arrived from the school to take me back. She was a woman who lived in the school and acted as secretary and messenger to the nuns. She also accompanied children who needed eye tests in the town She was not a likeable person, but I don't recall hating her.

I felt betrayed as we left Mrs Cunningham's, I had changed my mind about her. She was not a nice kind lady.

I remember how Sister Breeda enjoyed making me feel stupid about my escape. "Where did you think you were going?" she asked mockingly. She was aware of the fact that I had no idea of direction. I had told her that I was hoping to get to my mam. She asked me to tell her the exact route I had intended taking, she knew too well that I may as well be trying to reach Russia.

My third attempt at escape was triggered by having had a quarrel with Bernadette and my disgust at myself for having hit her and pulling her along the floor. I cannot even recall what caused it, but felt my sisters would be better off without me, and ran from the scene through the courtyard and headed towards the main gates via the farm.

Blinded by tears I ran frantically, getting back off the main road as quickly as possible. When my lungs hurt I stopped and sat down on the side of the road, wondering which way would take me to Dublin.

After walking for what seemed like an eternity, I looked for anything that looked edible along the hedgerows and was determined not to return to Summerhill. As on other occasions during self pity, I asked God why he had allowed kids like us to finish up in such awful places, believing that only bad people were put away. I not only felt abandoned by God and family, but most of all the people of Ireland. I had the same thoughts as we went out for walks on Sunday afternoons – I used to look at the houses along our walks and wonder why we could not live like the people within.

I did not see any familiar road signs; I suppose in my innocence I was looking for signs to Inchicore, Kimmage where Mam's family lived or even the North Strand. I knew that if I could spot a sign to Dublin that I could walk there and find most places where family lived.

Even though feeling hungry was normal in Summerhill, it felt worse not knowing when I would eat again. I had belly cramps but that could have been the result of what I picked from bushes and shrubs.

After sitting down and dozing off, I awoke feeling cold and worried, but kept walking. I had cried on occasions with mixed emotions of fear and thinking of my sisters. I was not totally surprised to find myself on the main road and opposite the little shop near the convent and realised I had gone in a complete circle.

As I walked down the little lane that ran along the top of Summerhill's playground I was reassured by the sound of the girls' chatter from beyond the hedge, but I had to study the situation before getting down on my belly and crawling under the gate. This was how I usually had to exit and enter on the occasions I went to the shop without permission. With permission I always went the long way there.

I had to move gradually, keeping my eyes peeled for any nuns or carers. I was still separated from the playground by the hedge that ran down the pathway which the nuns used to walk along, either praying or for exercise, and as I had no idea as to what time of day it was, there was always the chance I would be caught and punished.

I eventually joined the girls safely and was puzzled that nobody questioned where I had been, even though I was frequently sent to various jobs, someone must have questioned my empty place at dinner, which was at midday.

Our third meal, of a piece of bread and drink of cocoa arrived and eventually Sister Ursula stood as we all went to our dormitories but still there was no comment. I thought no more about it then, but on reflection wondered if it was possible that the nuns were using a different approach to my behaviour – I will never know!

I have no clear memory of apologising to Bernie nor would she expect me to. The hardest thing was that I had changed so much that I had hit my own sister, something I would have never done before coming to Summerhill.

The Bakery Dream

I envisaged the feast of my life when I was told to report to the bakery one day to help out. It was usually only the very trusted that was asked to do that work; I tried not to look over-excited.

The bakery was divided and the smaller end was called the creamery. The creamery was not as exciting as it sounds – it was where the butter was churned. I found it very tiring work as it was done manually. It was so tiring on the arms that we had to take turns.

I was surprised to see how large the loaves were, we had only ever seen the little cut-up chunks when served to us alternative mornings for breakfast and in the evening for tea. It was not looking promising, as the loaves were too big to shove one up a jumper or up a knicker leg.

Apparently the routine was the loaves would be left to cool overnight, cut up in the morning and sent over on wooden trays to Sister Breeda's kitchen, but we would not be doing the cutting. I decided that as we cleaned up and scrubbed the table, to appear to be closing the small windows but leaving one wedged so I could come back later and help myself.

I chose a time in the evening when I knew the nuns would go from prayer to supper and two of my friends and I slipped away from the group separately and met in the shrubbery outside the bakery windows past the farm.

I was given a lift up through the window and let myself down on to the small wooden chair below the window. I picked up two loaves and handed them to my friends outside and told them to wait for me before they started eating. I now had the risky bit – I needed to lock the window properly and exit through the door. It was a long way round to where my friends were waiting. I was going to have to run past the kitchen and hoped Sister Breeda had not gone to her kitchen between prayer and supper. My heart was thumping but my luck was in. After eating our fill we broke bits of bread and hid them on our person for family or close friends. We hid the remainder in the dense shrubbery for another feast the next evening. We returned the following evening at the same time and hoped that the overnight rain had not dampened our hoard.

Annie had got in trouble with Sister Ursula for not wearing her smock. We had taken the precaution of wrapping the remainder of the bread in it to keep insects out. We were so looking forward to another little feast, finding it hard to contain ourselves, but our excitement soon turned to horror on finding the navy-coloured bread soggy and not fit to eat. We never thought that the rain had been heavy enough to wet the bread, let alone Annie's smock dye running into it.

I have smiled many times during my life at risks I took for morsels of food. I am constantly reminded of life in Summerhill when I watch birds fighting for pieces of food and especially when lots of them peck and chase one little bird – exactly what would happen if we were ever unfortunate to drop food.

There are many girls who had spent their whole life in Summerhill who will not have perceived their treatment as I saw it, but as I have said before, they were so conditioned and would still fear the wrath of God for any criticism of the nuns or the clergy.

The Lesson On Life

It was some time after my fifteenth birthday when I and a few other girls were selected to attend the showing of a movie – the Sister in charge said it was to prepare us for life in the world outside.

I was quite excited at the prospect and took pleasure in bragging to other girls about it. These girls lost no time in telling us that we would probably only see a film showing us how to iron and do domestic duties. I gathered from those remarks that the girls were jealous that they were not selected especially as some of the girls were older than me, but to rub salt in the wounds I responded by saying that at least it was a sign that we would be getting out of the convent.

I had been an avid film freak before going into the convent and had seen every cowboy film that came to our local cinema. We were very bewildered after viewing the movie which told us how Saint Maria Goretti died, we had no idea what it had to do with life outside.

It was a silent film that started with people working in the fields making hay bales. It showed one girl in particular trying to avoid the attention of a young man who kept making eyes at her. It appeared she did not want to make friends with him and ignored his repeated attempts to get her to talk to him. Eventually the man knocked the girl down and after struggling quite a lot, the man stabbed her to death.

At the time we were supposed to understand that the girl had died to keep her virginity. The message we got from the film was that if a young man wants to befriend you and you continually refuse, he will stab you to death.

I honestly do not understand how the nuns expected us to have read any message into the film we had watched. We knew absolutely nothing about the birds and bees and the word 'virgin' was how we addressed the mother of God.

Personally I don't think there is anything wrong with a healthy fear of God – it keeps us on the straight and narrow, but Catholicism goes too far in its interpretation of Christian teaching.

I find it hard to accept that the same kind and loving God also condemns innocent little babies who die before baptism to eternity in limbo.

As a young child I had attended Mass on Sundays and Holy days but still had nightmares about dying in a state of mortal sin and spending eternity being poked and prodded with old Nick's poker in the fires of hell.

The nuns told us that Satin came in many disguises. I believe that the nuns had more in common with him than they did with God. Religious confusion can have a dreadful effect on the mind, and I am sure that it is the cause of many people ending up in asylums. In fact, I myself have struggled to keep my sanity. There were nights when I lay awake and tried to imagine what life would hold for me when my freedom came.

On reflection I feel so selfish about never giving a thought to what life in Summerhill would be like for my three younger sisters when I would no longer be around for them.

I had done the same about Leo. It appeared that somewhere along the line I had decided (though not consciously) that not talking about him would be less painful. I had even stopped asking Mam about how he was on her visits.

In reality, there was nothing I could do for him and knowing that when he reached a certain age that he would be sent to 'the dreaded Artane' was more than I could bear thinking of. I was not really sure who, if anyone, ever visited the poor little fellow and if the impression was given that kids in institutions had been abandoned by relatives it left them more likely to be abused.

I remember on the first two summer holidays and our names were not among those called out for home visits, I felt so abandoned. I was not to know that she had nowhere to take us and felt we had been forgotten, so if I could not understand at my age, what must be going on in my little brother's head or could he have forgotten us by this time.

I suppose I was getting to the stage of accepting that the fantasies I once had that some wealthy relative from America would come and claim us were got going to happen.

I had no way of knowing how difficult life was for our mam, I should have known that if there was a way to get us back, Mam would have found it.

The Holiday

As we sat there silently holding our breaths in the hope of hearing our names on the list of those whose families had requested them home for the summer holiday, I could not hide my delight on hearing mine and Bernie's names. On the first two summers that our names were not on the list, I could not begin to explain the feeling of pain I felt. We were not to know that here were genuine reasons why Mam could not have us and even though Sister Ursula would have been aware, she would not explain it to us. It might have helped.

Apparently Mam and Jim had to move twice in quick succession, and Mam had another two babies in between times. We later learned it was due to narrow-mindedness on the part of employers who were not happy about the fact that Mam and Jim were not married.

Anyway, Bernie and I were delighted that the summer of 1953 was our lucky break. Sheila and Betsy seemed to have forgotten about their life before Summerhill and did not share the same enthusiasm.

I was so happy to be in a house again with Mam, and I loved my new little sister and baby brother. I also liked the two boys and little girl my mam was now looking after. After the loss of their last accommodation Jim was forced to go into digs and Mam applied for a job as housekeeper to a man whose wife's job took her to America and his job was running a pub on the north side of Dublin. The man had no hesitation when Mam asked if she could bring her children to his house for the summer break – his only concern was how Mam could cope with nine children.

Sheila and Betsy were very quiet and bewildered with the strange children and clung to Bernie and I.

I helped Mam in every way I could, as did Bernie, at keeping them amused and the house cleaning. I got up early every morning just to make the days longer. Jim came at weekends to see Mam and his children, the little boy was very young.

Apart from helping care for the smaller children, Bernie and I also helped to clean the two rooms on the third floor of the house which was rented out to two men from the country whose work was in Dublin, their rooms were only done once weekly.

I suppose looking after my brother and sisters was much easier than the children of Mam's employers. They were a bit spoilt by their relatives who overcompensated for the absence of their mother, but on the whole they were likable kids.

On odd occasions Jim came and took Mam out for a couple of hours, but never for more than a couple of hours. It was always after the smaller ones were asleep which made baby-sitting easier for Bernie and myself. Bernie and I would chat about the events of the day – we were happy to be like a normal family.

I must have looked odd to the neighbours as I played with such little kids, because although we saw ourselves as big girls, Bernie and I were very childish compared to other fourteen and fifteen-year-olds.

We had found an old bicycle behind the shed and were having lots of fun in the yard and alleyway behind the house. We took turns in giving the younger kids rides while we held on to them.

We laughed and giggled with no thought of Summerhill. There was plenty of work and child minding to be done but it mattered little, it was all very enjoyable.

We saw very little of Mam's employer. He was a man of few words and did not interfere with Mam running the house. His children's ages ranged between three and seven, the older two were boys.

Apart from having just one parent, life was all it should be. We had no excess of any treats but we were happy. I could not explain the feeling of lying in bed at night under the same roof as Mam, not having to fear anyone – life was fun!

I never questioned why Mam never visited her family or took us to see them. In fact I wondered why they never volunteered to have any of us for a holiday, especially during the tough periods when Mam was not in a position to. I can only guess she would not ask help from the brothers and sisters who had so readily abandoned her in her time of need, but I suppose there were many like them who out of narrow-mindedness or rigid upbringing could not accept any fall from grace or indiscretions. I have to accept it was how things were back then.

Not in a million years could you have convinced Mam's family that any form of ill treatment or cruelty has taken place in convents. There were thousands like them and even today there are those who still hold the same blinkered views, and only in Ireland. I do believe that only time has helped me to understand.

The holiday with Mam in the North Strand ended all too soon and we were on the gloomy journey back to Summerhill, Athlone. Bernie and I were old enough to understand the reality, but Sheila and Betsy were just bewildered by our tears.

Christmas was now approaching and rumours of Government Policy on Industrial Schools was rife. God knows where the rumours originated, but there were some changes, such as plastic cups and saucers and plates followed by Formica-topped tables which would seat four people; there were also matching chairs.

These items were within the premises, but I was never to experience the change-over. Alas, I did not witness the improvement in dietary change either.

Surprises Were In Store

I was more than shocked to find that I was chosen to participate in the Christmas concert; so rehearsals for this would take my mind off the countdown to my 16th birthday on May 25th 1954, just months away.

I also recall us receiving the biggest parcel ever from Granny and Auntie Lily, it included a big Christmas cake amongst other things. Sister Ursula suggested we only take small amounts at a time.

I concentrated perfecting my steps for the Irish dancing I would be doing in the concert, though the biggest part was playing the bad King in the *Mikado*. I had taken an interest in the dancing as a way of listening to the gramophone, but I had begun to like it.

I was becoming very nervous as time drew nearer the concert and worried that I might be physically sick on the day. The problem with my stomach was that once it received food it would not give it back and the unproductive retching was very painful.

The part of the King was not my biggest worry, it was more the thought of not getting my steps right dancing to the live band from Athlone. We had only ever danced to the gramophone. I also had a dread of my knee-length socks slipping down.

To my amazement everything went fine during the *Mikado* and I really enjoyed the applause, even though there was some hilarity at my Japanese accent, but I had very few lines.

I remember looking at my reflection in the cloister window and thought I looked very smart in the hornpipe shoes and green sash across the front and green ribbon tied to hold up the knee socks.

Yes, one of the socks did slip during the dancing, but it didn't seem to matter with so much applause going on (which I believed was all for me). In reality the other two girls were really the stars – they were excellent, they had both danced from a very young age.

Most of the concert consisted of other girls either doing other dance arrangements or singing, but it was a very enjoyable time and if I remember correctly there were treats such as sweets and oranges sent from the Army base in Athlone Town. My surprise at taking part was not the only one in store for me.

The Big Surprise

With the concert over and Christmas on the horizon I was expecting that the time would drag between then and my release date. I could never have guessed what was in store for me on December 19th 1953 when Sister Ursula summoned me to her office.

She greeted me with one of her false smiles and handed me a bundle of clothing which included the red and lemon jumper I had knitted myself. "Put these on," she said and pointing to a pair of black shoes and stockings on the chair she told me to put those on too. There was no hint as to what was happening until I spotted Biddy Graeme – she was the older person that lived somewhere in the convent and ran all the errands for the nuns, including acting the job of escorting girls to and fro to various placements when they were released.

I had mixed feelings of excitement and fear, and even when Sister Ursula informed me that she was 'sending me out into the world' she had still not mentioned if I was to be farmed off to some rich Irish family or if I was lucky enough to be sent to Mam.

Apart from one change of clothing and a black crucifix with a white figure of Christ on it, I was given nothing else other than a short lecture on how to behave and make something of myself. We were halfway down the yard when I heard Bernie's voice from the door of the cloisters.

She was asking me where I was going and started to cry when I told her that I did not know, only that I was leaving. The picture of her standing there with her friend Mary upset me all the way into town.

I got the same reply from Biddy each time I enquired where I was going – "Wait and see."

As we had some time to kill before our train was due, Biddy informed me that we were going to wait in the home of someone she knew near the station in Athlone Town. The women in the house were very, very nice and made me tea and gave me cake while Biddy went and chatted to someone in the other room. I felt quite at home.

The delay was not too long and we were soon making our way along the tracks to God knows where. Biddy was reading a book and I was desperately trying to catch sight of familiar names on signs.

My geographical knowledge of Ireland was very limited, so I was none the wiser as to what direction we were heading. I did ask Biddy on occasions if we were going towards Dublin, but she carried on reading and telling me to just wait and see and grinned at my sighs of exasperation.

It was getting dark, limiting my view of the surrounding areas, but I was convinced that if we got to Dublin that it would be all lit up.

I eventually spotted the words *Baile Atha Cliath* and knew that was Gaelic for Dublin, but would not let Biddy see my excitement for fear of disappointment.

I knew that I could easily outrun Biddy and had decided that if we did not appear to be heading for the North Strand that I was going to abscond. She eventually asked me if I would be able to find where Mam lived on foot, or we could take a bus. I opted to walk.

I was excited and worried at the same time as I twisted the paper bag I was carrying with my spare set of clothes and the crucifix.

I was quietly praying that Mam had not moved since we were here on holiday with her, or perhaps her employer would say that I could not stay and Biddy would take me back to Summerhill – after all I would not be sixteen until May 25th, that was five months away and the court had said we would be released when we reached sixteen. My head was full of 'what ifs'.

My heart pounded as Mam answered the door in Nottingham street and we went into the hallway. I heard it said that I was out on a supervisory order and although I was polite to Biddy as she left to spend the night with friends in Dublin, I hoped never to see her again.

Mam's employer had said it was okay for me to be with her until I could find a job and get on my feet. This would not have been happening had Mam been cohabiting with Jim – he was still in digs and was still visiting Mam as before. Jim was still intending to go to England and find work as a farmhand with tied accommodation. The plan was still to send for Mam and his children; I was not part of the plan. I was to try and find an indoor job that would provide me with a room. On each visit to the house Jim would encourage Mam to get me sorted out and not let me get too comfortable.

Jim was doing little to endear me to him. Rejection was no stranger, but it still hurt. In my heart I knew I must find work but I desperately wanted to be near Mam and get to know her again.

Eventually he got his wish and I was taken to a very lovely house on the outskirts of Dublin for an interview. The job was as companion to the young daughter of the family. The house was beautiful with acres of land and its own tennis court.

It would have been a marvellous opportunity for someone who wanted to broaden their horizons, as the job would have taken me to foreign countries. I was like a chick, too young to leave the nest.

On the way back Mam tried to convince me of the marvellous opportunity the job would give me should I be offered it. I was to hear by letter if they thought me suitable. I hoped I would not be offered and cried many tears while I waited.

I was totally dependant on Mam for everything but she never made me feel like a burden.

Eventually the job was offered and I was in tears at the news. Mam did not force me to take it and wrote declining the offer. Jim was very angry and told Mam to keep trying.

I had written very little to my sisters and had kept none of the promises I made to them; but I was not likely to write letters of how hard life was, I knew the nuns read the letters and did not want them to know what the situation was, for fear of having to return. I was really beginning to see how hard life had been for Mam and realised why she could send us little or visit as often as I knew she wanted to. I could see now that she could not work miracles.

Soon after leaving Summerhill, I had written to Bernie promising her that she and the little ones would be having parcels from me. But nothing was working out as I had hoped, and with my worries of Jim taking Mam and the children to England, I was too busy trying to think of a way to stay with Mam.

I am not aware as to when Jim set off for England or being told that he had gone. The one incident I can recall was Mam having an argument with her employer. There were raised voices and the argument included the relatives who usually came to see Mr Coyle. I remember Mam packing our belongings after telling her employer to find someone else as housekeeper.

It was dark outside as we headed for the city, I had no idea where we would go and Mam was not saying much. I do not know how long we walked around before boarding a bus towards Ballyfermot. I could not imagine that Mam was going to go to our house which was now occupied by Dad and his new woman.

I had not been aware that Mam's old friend from Inchicore had been re-housed on the same estate and we ended up on her doorstep.

Lil still had family living at home and had very little room but she made us welcome. Angela her eldest child had been my closest friend when we lived in Inchicore, though we had little in common now, she seemed much more grown up than I was. I had no idea how long we could stay with Lil, and asked Mam if I could go and see my pal Bridie, the one close friend I had made after moving from Inchicore to Ballyfermot. Mam warned me not to go during daylight in case Dad spotted me. The last thing she needed was him knowing of her plight – he was not aware that I had been released from the convent.

My brother Danny knew, as he had visited us several times in the North Strand. Mam had been in contact with him even before I came out of Summerhill. My pal Bridie understood about the secrecy regarding my father.

The biggest shock was finding out that Mam had secretly arranged Danny's passage to England and he had joined Jim.

Even though it felt strange being on the same road (visiting Bridie) where I had once lived it was still lovely to see her. She lived on the opposite side of the road, close enough to my house to be seen if I visited during daylight.

I understood why Mam had kept Danny's departure so secret – I was aware of what would have happened had Dad heard of the plan, so the fewer people who knew the better! Mam had somehow made friends with a family just around the corner from Lil's house. I think Mam felt like she needed to give Lil her space whenever possible.

I will call Mam's new friends Mr and Mrs H. They had two little boys about five and six and were very nice people, and we would spend most of the day there at times, returning to Lil's at night.

Mam had been to the city to some organisation for help in our housing situation. I was not told of the outcome.

I used to play with the two boys and keep them amused while their mum got on with household jobs and was allowed to sit with Mam and Mr and Mrs H in the evening in front of their fire. I was always very tired due to the discomfort of the overcrowding and would sometimes fall asleep as they chatted.

I do not think our stay with Lil was as long a period as it felt, probably only a matter of days, but I was not to know due to the unforeseen circumstances that followed.

I had sat by Mam's chair as she talked to her friends and as usual I kept dozing off to sleep. As Mam decided it was time to go, Mrs H. suggested that I stay there the night – she said I could squeeze in the big double bed with the little boys who were fast asleep. It had to be more comfortable than Lil's floor.

I whipped off my shoes and skirt (I did not like fully undressing in strange houses), snuggled up behind the little chaps and was expecting to have a good night's sleep, but found it difficult to drop off – the landing light was left on and the door was ajar. I was very restless and could not go to sleep. I turned towards the wall as the landing light which was left on at night for the boys benefit was annoying, but the boys liked the door left ajar. After what seemed like an eternity I eventually dozed off, only to be woken by someone touching my chest.

My immediate reaction was to disturb the boy nearest to me by pinching his bottom. The shocked little fellow bolted upright, but was too sleepy to spot his daddy leave the room and go towards the lavatory. I was calming the youngster down as his mother came to investigate. She was immediately joined by her husband who claimed to have heard the boy call out as he had visited the lavatory. They seemed to accept that the child had a nightmare, apart from the feeling of fear at what happened. I also felt very ashamed at having pinched the sleeping boy. The older boy who was furthest away hardly budged, other than changing position.

I had to try and stay wide awake and get out of the house as soon as I saw daylight. It took ages before my heartbeat got back to normal and lots of things were going round in my head, I could not understand why the apparently nice man would want to do such a thing. I had thought of creeping out during the small hours, but then worried that Mr H. might pounce out at me.

After chewing the whole incident over in my head and wondering what Mam would say when I told her that I never wanted to sleep at the house again, I decided not to tell anyone.

I was the longest daybreak that I had ever waited for and I was never going to be able to talk to Mr H. again. I waited until Mr H. left the house for work and crept down the stairs and ran as fast as my legs could carry me.

I cried as I ran down Landen Road, feeling guilty about leaving Mam and my little sister and brother and could envisage Mam going around for me to the H. house. I knew I could get word to her that I was alright, but never the reason why I abandoned her.

Dad's door was opened by Alice who was surprised at my early call. She and Dad were now parents of a lovely little boy called Michael.

It was Saturday morning and Dad was doing overtime on the railway workshop where he worked.

I found myself telling Alice the whole story and begging her not to let Dad know of Mam's plight. I knew that I could trust this woman and I believe she understood that I could not bear the thought of Dad gloating at Mam's misfortune.

The story was, not to let Dad know that I had been living with Mam for months, but had just been released from the convent and Mam was employed in the North Strand as a live-in housekeeper and there was no room for me.

I really did hate this deceit, but with my father it was the only way to avoid an interrogation. I would also have to act surprised about Danno's departure.

Dad arrived from work after twelve o'clock and appeared quite pleased to see me, making no comment as to why I had no luggage other than what I stood up in. It was going to be a strain remembering not to let things slip that would indicate that I had been living with Mam – he would have expected me to come straight to him on my release from the convent.

Alice was definitely in agreement that Dad was never to know abut Mr H. She knew as well as I did, that the least Dad would have done would be to beat the man to a pulp and he would have accused Mam of putting me in moral danger.

Life Back With Dad

It did not take Dad long to decide what kind of job I would be suited to. I would be a machinist in a clothing factory. Of all the places in the world, I finished up with training from the nun's in Goldenbridge Convent. I don't know how Dad arranged it. There were no wages paid and I attended daily as though going to school, though not for so many hours.

I had plenty of time to get to know my little brother Michael. He was a lovely unspoilt child. I also saw much more of my friend Bridie, she was still my one and only friend.

I *never* attempted trying to contact Mam, I was sure that Jim had sent for her and the children by now and to be honest I was scared of going near the area for fear of ever seeing Mr H.

Sometimes after my sewing lesson I crossed over the nearby canal bridge and took the short cut to Gran's in Kimmage. Aunt Lily was now supplying me with all of my clothes and shoes – she loved to see me look nice.

The nuns soon helped me in finding a job in an English

Clothing Factory on the other side of the city. I immediately bought a new bike on credit.

Out of my wages of eighteen shillings Dad gave me back two shillings and sixpence, out of which I paid one shilling and sixpence off my bike. Uncle Dan used to visit every Saturday and gave me half a crown. This helped me to go the pictures a couple of times weekly, including Sunday afternoon at Chapolizard cinema. I am not sure if that's how it is spelt but that's how we pronounced it. I eventually had my wages reduced by three shillings when the boss decided that I was not going to make a machinist. I was kept on as a buttonholer and also soaped the inner lapels of the garments. I was also one of the young tea makers.

I was writing less to Bernie though I did feel very guilty now that there was a little happiness in my life.

Bad news reached me that Jim had not sent for Mam and she and the two little ones were living in a place for the homeless in James St. It was known locally as 'The Spike' – a place I never dreamed I would ever set foot inside.

Again I was going to keep secrets from Dad. I would go visit Mam on the pretence of visiting Gran. I cried quite a lot on my first visit. I had mixed emotions – happy that Mam was still in Dublin but very sad to see her reduced to this. The place was spotlessly clean but the families had no privacy. It looked exactly like a dormitory. Each bed had a locker and there were cupboards that people shared. They all had the use of the large laundry.

I could not bring myself to confide in Bridie about this, I felt so ashamed. I suppose for the same reason that I never spoke to anyone about my brother and sisters in the institutions. I have no idea why I should feel like this as we were not criminals. The only criminals were those in higher places who allowed this to happen to families.

It is sad to say that I was only able to deal with the incarceration of my brother and sisters by putting them to the back of my mind. It was strange that Mam never once asked why I had left her so suddenly, but she had known where I was; I never enquired as to how she found out.

I spent much of the visiting times with Mam, telling her about my job and my weekly routine. She wanted to know my every move and showed much interest in the fact that I did the weekly shopping every Friday evening for Dad.

I had no suspicions of her plans for me and was more than surprised one summer evening to be greeted by Bernie, and to my further surprise Mam was arranging for me to go to England and join Jim and my brother Danny. I had not complained of being dissatisfied with my life as it was, though I missed Mam. I went along with her plans.

Seeing and talking to Bernie was great and she dismissed my apology for not having kept my promise of parcels and letters. She told of the surprise at Sister Ursula allowing her out on holiday, especially in view of where Mam was living. I gave no thought as to why Sheila and Betsy were not allowed also.

I confided in Alice about where Mam was now living, but not about Bernie nor Mam's plans for me going to England and I felt dreadful about the deceit. She had been good to me and kept her promises of things I told her in confidence.

I had also become very fond of my little brother Michael and would miss him terribly when the time came for my departure.

The five pounds that Dad gave me weekly for the shopping was to be my fare to England. I did not possess many clothes and had been taking them a few at a time and leaving them with Mam.

Bernie was still on holiday with Mam when my departure evening came – she kept me amused with her face-pulling as Mam packed the little dark brown case; it was a very tatty old case, but the biggest embarrassment was the items that Mam was putting in it. Mam had said that Customs officers checked some baggage, but not everyone's. Bernie stood behind Mam, and was making all kinds of expressions as Mam placed her favourite old frying pan, followed by a square of waterproof material to prevent a child from wetting through to the mattress. Mam said it would cut down on the amount of stuff she would have to pack when she eventually followed me in the near future.

I said a tearful goodbye to Bernie as Mam accompanied me to the boat. Bernie was looking after the two little ones until Mam's return. I had presumed that Bernie would be returning to Summerhill in a very short time and had sent my regards to the little ones with more promises of what to expect when I got settled in England. I felt very emotional wondering when, if ever, I would see them again. Life, so far, had been all goodbyes.

It was with a feeling both of excitement and trepidation that I walked towards the boat that was to take me to another country and an uncertain future.

Mam appeared as nervous as I was as she checked that I had the piece of paper with Jim's address. She must have repeated that the place I was going to was halfway between a town called Luton and another town called Bedford, ten times or more.

I asked Mam if she was sure Jim would not be angry at my arrival – after all, we were never good friends. Her reply that he would have to get used to it was not very reassuring. I comforted myself with the thought of my brother Danny as an ally.

Suddenly I was looking at the boat and hugging Mam goodbye, both of us snivelling!

I felt so alone and awkward, even though I was surrounded by lots of people boarding, but they all appeared as though they had done it many times before. I was wishing that the feel of Mam's last hug had not faded so quickly.

I was fighting back tears and choking on the large lump in my throat, I felt so tiny on this very large boat.

I found myself a corner on deck and tried thinking of as many funny situations that I had been in – anything to cheer myself up. I sat and looked many times at the scrap of paper with Jim's address and thought about the funny faces Bernie had made behind Mam's back as she had packed my case, but none of the funny memories had the desired effect for long, I still felt lost.

The Boat Journey To England

I felt quite relieved when the boat moved away from the dock. I was convinced that Dad would have guessed why I had been gone so long for the weekly shopping and had been half expecting to be found and dragged off the boat! But my conscience did bother me for the way I had left without goodbyes to some special people in my life.

It was good thinking that I had found a secluded place to sit on my own – it would spare me having to talk to anyone, not only because Mam had told me not to talk to strangers, but the nuns had done a good job too in scaring the daylights out of me.

Sitting huddled on my own left plenty of time for reflection. I wondered if I would ever again see my brothers and sisters whom I was leaving behind.

I was very tearful again and the lump was back in my throat and not having warm clothes meant I was too cold to fall asleep. I gave little consideration to how my father would react – would he assume Alice could have been involved? He had never made any comments after Danny had disappeared, it was never discussed. Even if Alice was grilled, she was not as scared of Dad as Mam had been. I suppose I convinced myself that all would be forgotten. I believe that Danny had witnessed violence towards Alice during the period after our incarceration and he had lived with them, but I had not seen this during my short stay with them. I did think that in my short life, of how much had gone on; a very short space of time had seemed like an eternity.

I was feeling cold now and wished I possessed a coat. I stood the case on its end and tried shielding myself behind it. At first I had laid it in a way as to prevent anyone from sitting near me, not realising there would be few who would want to be in such a cold draughty place.

I urgently needed to visit the lavatory but worried that someone might remove my case while I was away, though looking back now I laugh at the thought of the look on any would-be thief on opening the case. I would probably have received a donation.

I eventually had to move; my feet were so numb that I could barely move them, it was a chilly night. When I finally found the toilets my thoughts returned to Summerhill Convent – the floors were full of urine from overflowing toilets; not only was I cold on returning to my cold spot but my feet were also wet.

Daylight was breaking when I was approached by a smart lady who came out for a stroll on deck. She told me she was a writer for an English magazine, she left after giving me a bar of Cadburys chocolate. I was so hungry that I could have eaten it with the wrapper on.

The lady must have thought that I was very rude as I had only used the words 'yes' and 'no' to her questions, but the nuns had instilled much fear in our minds – the warning that the devil came in many disguises came to mind often. It may sound foolish but we took everything they said literally.

The journey must have been one of the loneliest times of my life.

The next surprise was the length of the train journey to London, but at least it was much more cosy and I was much more at ease, having found myself a carriage all to myself. Mam's last message was to keep to myself and only ask the way from ladies, and on no account allow anyone to lead me off anywhere at London stations.

I was sitting deep in thought wondering what sort of welcome I would get from Jim and what sort of place Barton was, when the train slowed down. I could not see a station but was not worried why we had slowed down, when the door opened and a dirty-faced man came into the carriage.

I sat petrified and choked on my reply as the man asked me if I was alright. Why I thought, did he have to choose this carriage? I felt sick to the pit of my stomach and my throat was thumping as well as my heart – I wondered if he could hear the pounding!

He had obviously picked up on my accent and asked if I was a Colleen and after acknowledging that he was right, found myself babbling on like a record.

I told him that my big brother would be waiting for me at the station. This was not true as I was to be met at Luton station. I had been studying Mam's instructions which she had written down for me but kept them tightly in my hand for fear he would ask to read them and find out that I had fibbed.

I don't really know why I talked so much, perhaps it had something to do with my comprehension of the violent death of St. Maria Goretti, after all my view of the film was that she died because she would not speak to the man who tried to befriend her.

On reflection, the man must have been glad to get off the train to give his ears a rest. I was so relieved when the train again slowed down and the man (who turned out to be a rail worker) got off the train. How could I have known that it was his usual routine?

It's strange now when I look back, that I never told anyone I ever met, that I had spent time in a children's home.

I bet the ordinary workman would never guess the fear his presence in that rail carriage had instilled in the heart of this ignorant Irish Colleen.

Suddenly people were shuffling about and gathering up their belongings, so obviously the train was nearing its destination.

Most people were accompanied, but those who were alone appeared to me to know exactly where they were going. I envied them. My sense of direction in my country of birth was bad enough, how was I going to manage in this strange land?

I spotted the lady who had given me the bar of chocolate and asked for her help. She put me at ease by directing me to St. Pancras, telling me that my journey to Luton or Bedford was only thirty minutes or so.

I was very tired as I journeyed toward Luton and struggled to keep my eyes open. I was fearful of missing my stop.

I felt very alone again as people went their way at Luton station. Danny had not come to meet me, as I had hoped.

I approached the guard and asked him if he could guide me to the address written on my piece of paper only to be told that I should have stayed on the train and on to Bedford.

I had little money and asked the guard if I would have to pay again. He was quite helpful and put me on the next train to Bedford, explaining to the station inspector who was getting on the train that I had got off the train too soon. I felt tearful again as I sat down and even began to wish that I was back in Ballyfermot. I was cold and very hungry, but dare not spend any money in case I should need it for travel.

On arriving at Bedford I sought the help of a lady who was just about to catch a bus. She in turn passed me over to a gentleman (who happened to be Irish). The man assured me he knew the road well, took hold of my case and told me to follow him. Unfortunately the man had read the address as Shakespeare Road and not Sharpenhoe, so once again I was at the bus station and was helped by a lady who was actually going my way.

The lady was kind enough to explain to the conductor that I was to be let off in Barton Village and from there anyone would know the road I needed.

The lady got off at a place called Silso and made a point of reminding the conductor to let me off at 'The Oak' pub.

As the cream bus pulled away I noticed 'Birch Bros' on the side, I had been too anxious and tired when I had got on to notice anything, other than it was a bus.

At last I was standing next to a road sign marked 'Sharpenhoe Road' and, as my luck would have it, it was (according to the lady) a very long road and the number I needed was at the furthest end.

A long Road it was, but it was the right Road!

January 23rd 1996

Soon after finishing the account of our lives, I discovered that my favourite nun, Sister Incarnata, was still alive and living in Castlerea. I lost no time in writing and was delighted to receive a reply. I was quite surprised she remembered my family so clearly. She mentioned my sad life and how much good she knew was in me. She mentioned how she had encouraged me to write. Unfortunately she passed away within a very short time of making contact.

I had also been in contact with two girls who were in Summerhill during my time there. One whose memory of me was vague, though mine of her is crystal clear. I have not kept in touch with her but the other girl Patty and I write and exchange cards at Xmas.

My younger sister has kept in touch with several girls and has been over to visit one. She and Sheila spent their full time within the convent until they were sixteen.

I have heard of two girls from Summerhill who disliked each other strongly only to find out after leaving that they were sisters.

Another girl found out after leaving that her mother had come from a short distance from the convent. She also found a sister she did not know existed who lived in Dublin – her mother had lived in England but died before she made contact.

I will never understand the cruelty of the nuns and the Irish Government of that period. Some girls were lucky on finding family that they were able to form a bond, but many never did. Separating siblings can be very destructive to families. I have not been lucky enough to find anyone who knows the whereabouts of my closest pals. Perhaps they put as much distance between themselves and Ireland as possible depending on how bad the nightmares are, though running is not the answer, they cannot be shaken off.

June 1997

At last during a holiday to Ireland, Bernie and I were persuaded by my husband to face our ghosts and visit Summerhill.

Bernie was not keen, it was difficult enough to get her to talk about our past, but I had always wanted to equate the appearance of the place with the description I had written about from memories of forty or more years ago.

I did not recall ever seen the statue of St. Joseph in the playground and the windows of the school building appeared lower than I remembered. The whole sight made me feel sick and I wondered why I was putting myself through this.

I took my husband to show him the bakery window from where I had stolen the loaves all those years ago. Again the windows seemed lower. It was hard to believe I had found it so difficult to climb. The bushy shrubbery was no longer there.

Bernie was very quiet and I began to wonder if it had been a mistake to come here.

The grotto was still standing in the same place, but this time I did not pray as I passed. We decided we had seen enough and went towards Drum cemetery. I was going to keep the promise I had made to myself many times and pray for Mary Biddy.

I cannot describe my feelings on seeing her name on the large headstone. Hers was the last name on the stone – the dates went back over a hundred years.

It does not bear thinking about as to what kind of treatment some of those poor girls must have suffered during their lives. I touched every letter of Mary Biddy's name and spoke to her silently. She was actually eighteen-and-a-half and not nineteen as I had guessed in writing my account.

I could not help the feeling of extreme anger as, on leaving, I spotted the highly decorated grave of a member of the IRA. I did not regard it as fitting that he should share the same resting place as those innocent girls who had never felt the hand of friendship or love from their own countrymen or women.